Mapping the Dharma

A Concise Guide to the Middle Way of the Buddha

Mapping the Dharma

A Concise Guide to the Middle Way of the Buddha

Paul Gerhards

Parami Press
Vancouver, Washington

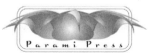

Parami Press

Published by
Parami Press
13023 NE Hwy 99, Ste. 7, #193
Vancouver, Washington 98686

Library of Congress Catalog Number: 2006934074
ISBN: 978-0-9779774-0-6

Printed in the United States of America

Cover design by Another Jones Graphics, Portland, Ore.
Cover illustration by the author

With gratitude and loving kindness I thank my Dhamma friend, Ajahn Chandako, Abbot of Vimutti Monastery, Bombay, New Zealand, whose hours of patient assistance helped me understand and express many of the finer points of Buddhist doctrine. To Ajahn Chandako, *añjali*.

To Robin,
for her
help
patience
guidance
support
love
and title
of this book

May all beings benefit from the merits of this work.

Contents

Section 4: The Factors of the Path in Detail—49

Section 5: Further Definitions—67

Appendices—95

Glossary—108

Index—112

Introduction

Although he lived 2,500 years ago, the Buddha's teachings are as universal now as they were then. The Buddha taught for 45 years until his death in about 486 BCE—enough time to speak many millions of words. He often organized his talks around lists of concepts and qualities as a means to make his point to a variety of audiences so his teachings could be easily understood and memorized. Held within these scriptures are collections of lists categorized as the Book of the Ones, the Book of the Twos, all the way to the Book of the Elevens.

Indeed, the Dharma (the Buddha's teachings) was passed on verbatim for centuries as an oral tradition before the teachings were written during the first century BCE. Accurate transmission of the teachings relied not only on the lists but also on repetition. Most of the longer Buddhist scriptures are filled with phrases that repeat several times, with subtle variations.

The Four Noble Truths form the foundation of a profound way of viewing the world and living within it. When I began my journey into Buddhism as a means to spiritual and personal growth, I was both intrigued and confused by the many lists that presented themselves to me. I wanted to know and understand as much as I could. But at first the more I learned, the more muddled I got. I wanted some order, some structure to follow.

The teachings of the Buddha—the Dharma—are not static and cannot be held within a rigid container. The Dharma is the totality of the Buddha's teachings and its constituent parts. The parts interact and overlap with one another to form a logical step-by-step procedure for attaining full and complete understanding of the nature of reality. However, one need not perfect one aspect before moving on to the next; rather, one simply begins to practice meditation and study the Dharma. In time the parts begin to coalesce and one sees just how each aspect supports the others and how the Dharma fits into every moment of the day.

Still, as a student of the Dharma, what I found useful was a structure to help me see how the teachings fit together. *Mapping the Dharma* began as a collection of lists compiled, as I came across them, in a file called "By the Numbers." It wasn't long before I thought it would be helpful to visually link some of the more important lists. This book is the result. What I hope to have achieved is a visual guide to the teachings—more a map than a text.

The Buddha said that a map is not the territory; it is merely a tool of discovery. He said the same about the Dharma: It is a tool that enables the practitioner to become fully awake.

For the novice, language is another source of confusion surrounding the various Buddhist lists. The scriptures were orally transmitted first and later written in Pali, the language of the common people of the area. Today, Pali is the language of the Theravada tradition, and Sanskrit is used by the the Mahayana tradition of Buddhism. (For brief descriptions of these traditions, see Appendix C.)

Although Pali and Sanskrit are similar, differences in spelling may lead to misunderstanding for the beginner who reads from a variety of sources. A primary example is the widely used Sanskrit word *dharma*. In Pali, the word is *dhamma*. Two other commonly used Sanskrit words are *karma* and Nirvana. In Pali, they are *kamma* and Nibbana. I use the Sanskrit forms of these words in the book, but, unless otherwise noted, I indicate a few Pali equivalents for some English words.

Many words and concepts from both languages do not translate well into English. It's not unusual for different translators to use a variety of English synonyms for a single Pali or Sanskrit word. An example is the Pali word *pañña*, which can mean "wisdom" or "discernment." When hearing or reading these English renderings, a beginner may think the speaker or writer is talking about two different concepts, which may or not be true depending on the context. One source may use wisdom, whereas another may use discernment but with no contextual difference in meaning.

Some Buddhist words have multiple meanings. Again I use dharma as an example. In one context, used with a capital *D* it means the teachings of the Buddha. When used with a lower-case *d,* it could refer to the way things are or, in its plural form, simply *things*.

Another word that does not translate well into English is *dukkha*. The standard rendering is "suffering." Suffering, in its most mundane sense, is easy to understand because everyone suffers pain and anguish at one time or another.

Dukkha, however, refers to all forms of suffering, from the slightest dissatisfaction and discomfort to the most severe physical and emotional pain. Furthermore, and most important, dukkha refers to the subtle but inherent unsatisfactoriness of things. In other words, nothing short of Nirvana has the ability to fully satisfy. Anything less is dukkha

All references to suffering, then, should be understood in this way.

How to Use this Book

Mapping the Dharma: A Concise Guide to the Middle Way of the Buddha is easy to use, but the reader also may find it easy to get sidetracked while wandering through its pages. There are two reasons. First is the nature of the Buddha's teaching itself. Following the Middle Way begins with a desire to end one's suffering based on an understanding of the causes of that suffering. It ends with the realization of the goal—liberation. Yet the Noble Eightfold Path is not something to be mastered one step at a time before moving to the next. Rather, the teachings are practiced and, with patience and persistence, mastered simultaneously over time.

This leads to the second reason you may find yourself wandering back and forth through this book rather than making a linear path through it. *Mapping the Dharma* is not laid out in a strictly sequential order. As the title suggests, this is a book of maps, an atlas, so to speak. The maps you'll find on these pages don't depict physical places, but concepts.

Just as an atlas of road maps may have you skipping from one place to another. *Mapping the Dharma* will have you skipping from one concept to another. In both cases what's important are the relationships among the destinations, not the order in which they appear.

Mapping the Dharma attempts to depict the relationships among the key concepts of the Buddha's teachings while offering concise explanations of these aspects along the way.

Some concepts—the Four Noble Truths, for example—are logically superior in order of appearance to others. Instead of laying out the book in a hierarchical fashion, however—with one key topic and its subordinate ideas presented one after the other before moving on to the next key topic—I have grouped key topics together with references pointing to subordinate concepts explained in other parts of the book.

In the body of the book are two kinds of references to look for. A large signpost at the top of the page containing an up arrow, a topic, and a page number refers you to that superior topic discussed on a preceding page.

A smaller signpost at the bottom of a page contains a down arrow, a topic, and a page number. This refers you ahead to a subordinate list or an explanation of a specific topic.

Appendix A: The Maps at a Glance presents an overview of the book's structure. These maps illustrate on a reduced scale the relationship among all the factors presented here.

Author's note: The maps form the framework of the book. The lists are organized hierarchically and, in most cases, adhere to a time-honored structure. In some cases, however, other arrangements may be possible.

Section 1

Going for Refuge

Taking Refuge in the Three Jewels

To follow the path of the Buddha is to take refuge in the Three Jewels—the Buddha, the Dharma, and the Sangha.

Upon his awakening, the Buddha discovered the path to Nirvana and complete freedom from pain and suffering. To take refuge in the Buddha means to have faith that the Buddha actually experienced this freedom as the Fully Awakened One and that he, as teacher and guide, can lead us to the same end.

The Dharma is the teachings of the Buddha. To take refuge in the Dharma means to explore the teachings, practice them well, and see whether the practice leads to the reduction in—even the end of—all forms of suffering.

The Sangha refers to the ordained monks *(bhikkhus)* and nuns *(bhikkhunis)* who follow the path of the Buddha. On a higher level, it refers to all those, past and present, who have followed the path fully to awakening. To take refuge in the Sangha is to recognize that ordinary human beings following the Buddha's way can become fully awakened beings in this lifetime. The Sangha gives support to all who walk the Path of Peace. The Sangha is their support.

In long-ago India ordinary people would take refuge in a patron, landowner, king, teacher, or god to protect them from harm and from the miseries of life. Although we are miles away in space and time from the days of the Buddha, suffering still comes to us in many forms from the not-so-subtle upsets and tragedies to the almost unnoticed everyday irritations that befall each of us moment by moment.

The Buddha gave the world a refuge and pointed the way out of the cycle of pain and suffering. He invited us to take a look, try out his teachings, see for ourselves whether they work. Buddhism is free of dogma and compulsion. None of the teachings need be accepted on faith alone. Buddhism is not about belief or blind faith, but about doing. The Middle Way is a way of life lived within the framework morality and generosity.

In taking refuge in the Three Jewels we see that through our own effort, liberation from suffering is possible.

Traditional Pali Chants of Paying Homage and Taking the Three Refuges

Namo tassa bhagavato arahato sammasambuddhassa

Homage to the blessed, noble and perfectly enlightened one
(Repeated three times)

Buddham saranam gacchami
Dhammam saranam gacchami
Sangham saranam gacchami

To the Buddha I go for refuge
To the Dharma I go for refuge
To the Sangha I go for refuge

Dutiyampi buddham saranam gacchami
Dutiyampi dhammam saranam gacchami
Dutiyampi sangham saranam gacchami

For the second time, to the Buddha I go for refuge
For the second time, to the Dharma I go for refuge
For the second time, to the Sangha I go for refuge

Tatiyampi buddham saranam gacchami
Tatiyampi dhammam saranam gacchami
Tatiyampi sangham saranam gacchami

For the third time, to the Buddha I go for refuge
For the third time, to the Dharma I go for refuge
For the third time, to the Sangha I go for refuge

The Three Jewels

Buddha

Dharma

Sangha

Page 21
Buddha

Page 23
Dharma

Page 24
Sangha

Buddha

The Buddha was born Siddhartha Gautama, a prince of the Sakya clan in what is now Nepal, in about 563 BCE. He belonged to the class of warriors and aristocrats. At birth, prophecy held that he would become either a great king or a great spiritual teacher. To ensure that he would follow the proper path of his class, Gautama's father sheltered his son from the realities of life. He built three palaces where the boy was lavished with pleasure, luxury, and privilege.

As a young man, Gautama married Yashodhara and had a son, Rahula. When Gautama was about 29 years old, he ventured with his attendant into the world at large. He saw four people who changed the direction of his life. The first person was a very old man. The second was a sick person. The third was a corpse. Living always within the confines of his palaces, Gautama had never encountered such strange and disturbing images. They troubled him deeply. He asked his attendant if his own fate included first aging, then sickness, and then death. The answer each time was yes; aging, sickness, and death are inescapable for all, even a prince.

The fourth person Gautama saw was a wandering mendicant. In Gautama's time many renounced the worldly life for a life of meditation and practices of austerity as a means to higher spiritual purpose and understanding. When Gautama saw the wanderer, he was deeply moved by the man's peaceful and happy demeanor in spite of his poverty.

Reflecting on those four meetings, and understanding that riches and high birth would not protect him from sickness, old age, and death, Gautama wondered if living in the opposite extreme would, and he determined that he would renounce his life of luxury for one of austerity. He left the refuge of the palace, shed his royal robes, and donned the rags of a seeker. His goal was to discover nothing less than the end of suffering.

For six years the Bodhisattva (Buddha-to-be) Gautama wandered the countryside, practicing austerities alone or with other seekers. Contemporary wisdom held that depriving the body was the means to spiritual fulfillment; legend said that the Buddha was able to reduce his diet to one grain of rice or one tiny fruit a day. He became so emaciated, it is said, that he could touch his spine by placing his fingers on his belly.

While bathing in a river one day, and weak from fatigue and malnutrition, he fell and nearly drowned. Resting and reflecting beneath a tree, he decided to take some nourishment and regain his health. He realized there was no value in extreme asceticism, that it was no more the means to the end of suffering than was the opulence of palace life. He could go no further on that path.

Still, the Bodhisattva Gautama was determined to find a way he could escape the cycle of suffering. There had to be something between the extremes of opulence and austerity that would point the way. One evening he sat at the foot of a tree to meditate. He vowed not to arise until he found what he had sought.

And so he did. A universe of knowledge revealed itself, and the Bodhisattva became the Buddha, the Awakened One, the Tathagata, the one who attained the highest spiritual goal. That night the Buddha saw thousands of his own past lives. He saw the workings of karma throughout the many lives of other beings, throughout "eons of expansion and contraction." He saw the truth of the nature of suffering and the cause of suffering in the world. He understood that ordinary human beings—regardless of class—were capable of ending suffering through their own efforts. And, finally, he formulated the means of ending suffering—even the suffering of birth and death.

When the Buddha came out of meditation, he decided to keep his knowledge to himself, thinking that no one would be able to comprehend all that had come to him. But a *deva,* a radiant being from a higher plane of existence, saw what was in the mind of the Buddha. "Surely," the deva implored, "there are those with little dust in their eyes" who would benefit from this newly discovered knowledge. The Buddha relented and agreed to instruct others.

He then sought the five companions with whom he had recently practiced austerities. They initially rejected the Buddha, believing he had gone soft, had gone back to the worldly life. But they also noticed a peaceful radiance they had not seen before. They let him speak.

The Buddha told them of his discovery. The first Dharma talk, the *Dhammacakkappa-vattana Sutta,* is known as the "Discourse on Setting in Motion the Wheel of Dharma." The Buddha taught that liberation could not be attained through the accumulation of wealth and indulgence in sensual pleasures, nor could it be found in the practice of self-affliction and extreme deprivation. Both practices were ignoble and unprofitable and should be avoided. The path to liberation was the Middle Way of the Eightfold Path, which is the fourth of the Four Noble Truths.

Dharma

Dharma refers to the teachings of the Buddha. But the word has many other meanings, among them "the way things are," "truth," or "the true nature of things." It can also mean "phenomenon," "thing," and "object of mind." And it can mean "everything that is," including the "unconditioned." The *unconditioned* refers to that which has no prior cause or condition. The unconditioned is Nirvana itself. When we explore the Dharma, we explore all these things, and our exploration begins with the Four Noble Truths.

The Four Noble Truths

Page 26
Four Noble Truths

Sangha

While the Buddha was teaching in the world, the ordained monks and nuns who were his disciples were referred to as the *Sangha*. A different word, *parisa,* was used for the assembly of lay followers and benefactors who supported the Sangha. After the Buddha's death, the Sangha continued to grow, initially without a leader. But before his death he had told them the *Dhamma-Vinaya,* his teachings and monastic code would be their guide.

The role of the Sangha is to keep the teaching alive for the benefit of all beings. As one of the Three Jewels, the Sangha as Refuge—*strictly speaking*—refers to the community of Noble Beings, past or present, who have attained or realized one of the four stages of the spiritual path.

The first stage is that of that of Stream-winner, one who is free of the first three of ten afflictions known as the Ten Fetters that bind one to the world: the misunderstanding that there is an individual, **separate personality** (self); **skeptical doubt** in the Dharma; and the belief that **rites and rituals** in and of themselves are means to spiritual attainment. The Stream-winner is so firmly established in the Dharma that full awakening is guaranteed within seven lifetimes and is no longer subject to rebirth in a lower realm.

The Once-returner, in addition to being free of the first three fetters, is *nearly* free of the next two—**sensuous craving** and **ill-will**—and is assured of only one more rebirth in a human or lower heavenly realm, during which lifetime suffering will end.

The Non-returner is *fully* free of the first five afflictions and will not return again to this world.

The *Arahant* is fully free of the five remaining fetters: craving for **fine-material existence** and **immaterial existence,** and **conceit, restlessness,** and **ignorance.** An Arahant is a fully awakened being whose realization of Nirvana is complete. An Arahant, however, is not a buddha.

Sometimes these beings are referred to as the Eight Pairs of Noble Beings, e.g., Stream-winners and those established on the path to Stream-winner, and so on.

To take refuge in the Sangha ultimately means to rely on those who have attained the highest levels of spiritual practice. Conventionally speaking, it refers to the community of fully ordained monks and nuns.

In contemporary Western usage Sangha has come to mean "community of practitioners," including lay practitioners. Used as such it refers to groups who may gather regularly to practice meditation together. Although this unorthodox usage will likely stick, it should be understood that taking Refuge in the Sangha does not mean taking refuge in any group of practitioners.

Section 2

The Four Noble Truths

**Dharma
Page 23**

The Four Noble Truths

The Four Noble Truths are called noble because they are practiced and understood by those who would renounce worldly gain for the sake of a higher spiritual purpose. The first truth—suffering—is to be comprehended. The second truth—the cause of suffering—is to be eradicated. The third truth—the end of suffering—is to be realized. The fourth truth—the way—is to be developed.

The formula of the Four Noble Truths is often compared to that of a doctor treating a patient. First, the doctor is presented with a disease or other ailment. Next the doctor determines the cause of the affliction. With the disease and cause understood, a determination can be made as to a cure. Finally, the doctor prescribes the cure and presents a plan for recovery.

To apply the components of comprehension, eradication, realization, and development contained within this formula is to practice the Dharma, to walk the Middle Way.

Suffering
The Cause of Suffering
The End of Suffering
The Way to the End of Suffering

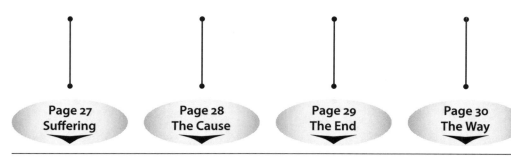

**Page 27
Suffering**   **Page 28
The Cause**   **Page 29
The End**   **Page 30
The Way**

The Four Noble Truths
Page 26

The First Noble Truth: Suffering

Suffering, called *dukkha* in both Pali and Sanskrit, includes any form of mental or physical pain or stress, from the smallest irritation to grief, sorrow, and death itself. It is the nature of all beings to experience dukkha in their lives.

Although everyone experiences unhappiness once in a while, and many are truly miserable much of the time, we don't generally *comprehend* we are suffering—especially when things seem to be going just fine. Instead, we see ourselves as unlucky, or oppressed, or victims of circumstance, or simply annoyed by one thing or another. Suffering, then, must be seen for what it is before it can be dealt with effectively.

All suffering can be put into one of three categories:

Ordinary Suffering

Suffering of Change

Suffering of Conditioned Existence

Page 68
Kinds of Suffering

The Four Noble Truths
Page 26

The Second Noble Truth: The Cause of Suffering

The Buddha teaches that craving *(tanha)*—in any form and to any degree—and ignorance *(avijja)* are the causes of suffering. For suffering to end, craving and ignorance must be *eradicated* from our lives.

It is the nature of being human to experience pain, grief, lamentation, sickness, old age, and death as well as many other afflictions. Suffering arises when we desire—*crave*—things to be different from what they are. It is this constant grasping for satisfaction, enforced by a fundamental inability to recognize dissatisfaction in its many forms, that brings suffering into our lives.

Like suffering, craving can be placed into one of three categories, as illustrated on page 31. There is, however, but one form of desire the Buddha found to be praiseworthy: the desire for awakening *(dhamma-chanda)*. It is this desire that leads one to practice the Middle Way and bring suffering to an end.

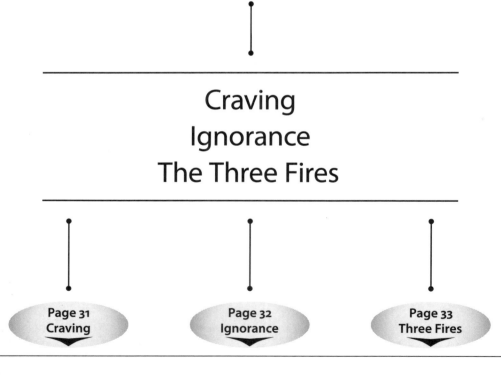

Craving

Ignorance

The Three Fires

Page 31
Craving

Page 32
Ignorance

Page 33
Three Fires

The Four Noble Truths
Page 26

The Third Noble Truth: The End of Suffering

With a firm understanding of the Three Characteristics of Existence—that all conditioned things are **impermanent, unsatisfactory,** and **without an enduring substance** (p. 50)—we can begin to let go of conditioned phenomena. These insights will lead to disenchantment with the world, to dispassion so as to be rational and impartial, and to the cessation of ignorance and craving. With the cessation of all forms of clinging, one realizes Nirvana: the unconditioned, the deathless.

This is the Buddha's discovery, *that the end of suffering is possible in this lifetime,* in the here and now. With effort one can achieve—can *realize*—this goal. The Sangha is testimony to the possibility.

Nirvana

Page 34
Nirvana

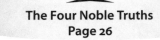

**The Four Noble Truths
Page 26**

The Fourth Noble Truth: The Way to the End of Suffering

The Fourth Noble Truth is the Buddha's Middle Way, the path to the cessation of craving and ignorance. This way is called the Noble Eightfold Path. This is no ordinary path, however, with a beginning at Point A and ending at Point B. Rather, it is a collection of interrelated qualities that must be *developed* alongside one another in order to make progress along the way.

Developing these qualities takes time. It also takes motivation. After all, if we do not want to end suffering, then we won't take the necessary steps to do so. This is entirely a choice one makes on one's own. There is no compulsion. And there is no punishment for not following the path. But, as always, there *is* suffering. And there always will be suffering unless one is motivated to make an end of it.

The Noble Eightfold Path

**Page 36
Eightfold Path**

The Second Noble Truth
Page 28

Craving

Craving, which is a result of ignorance, is the cause of all suffering in ourselves and in the world. Craving, or thirst, is any kind of wanting, whether it's craving *for* something or craving *not* for something. Craving causes suffering because with craving comes attachment. The very nature of attachment is the inability to let go, which creates tension because of our desire to keep things from changing, an impossibility.

Our failure to understand the correlation between craving and suffering (or ignoring the connection when we do understand) is, by definition, ignorance.

Craving for Sensual Pleasure

Craving for Existence

Craving for Nonexistence

Page 69
Craving

The Second Noble Truth
Page 28

Ignorance

Ignorance clouds the mind, which prevents us from seeing the true nature of things. Because of ignorance we cling to the notions of permanence and stability, satisfaction and self-gratification, and that we have an unchanging and eternal essence that can be identified as "I," or "me," or "mine." As such ignorance is the root cause of all suffering and evil because greed and hatred are both rooted in ignorance.

Of what are we ignorant? We are ignorant of the true nature of the way things are. Nothing that arises through causes and conditions—and that is everything except Nirvana, which has neither cause nor conditions—is permanent or stable, nothing is inherently satisfying for very long, and all things are insubstantial and void of what can be called a "self."

Ignorance is defined as not knowing and fully understanding the Four Noble Truths: suffering, the cause of suffering, the possibility to bring an end to suffering, and the way to bring about the end of suffering. When the Four Noble Truths are fully understood and the Noble Eightfold Path mastered, ignorance is dispelled.

The Second Noble Truth
Page 28

The Three Fires

The Three Fires are analogous to craving and ignorance as the root causes of suffering. They are the three states of mind that leave us confused and—until they are expunged—destined to wander in darkness.

The fires of greed, hatred, and delusion affect all our decisions and actions. Even when we firmly believe in the "rightness" of our actions, so long as our decisions are influenced by any of the fires, suffering will result.

The fires reinforce one another as they establish themselves in our psyche and influence our lives and the lives of those around us. Any time one of the fires influences behavior, we create more suffering for ourselves and likely for others as well.

Greed

Hatred

Delusion

Page 70
Three Fires

The Third Noble Truth
Page 29

Nirvana

The word Nirvana (Nibbana in Pali) means extinction or to be extinguished. In the Buddha's day, fire was thought to be a part of its fuel. A log burned, for example, because the fire was *bound* to it. When the fire went out—was *extinguished*—it became unbound, released from the log.

This example of unbinding is how Nirvana can be understood. Beings are bound to *samsara*—the wheel of suffering and pain—by the fires of greed, hatred, and delusion. When—through ardent practice of the factors of the Noble Eightfold Path—greed, hatred, and delusion are extinguished, the practitioner becomes unbound from samsara and is free from suffering.

Nirvana, then, is not a place. It is a state of being that simply *is*. Nothing causes it to come into being and nothing can cause it to cease to be. Other names for Nirvana include the unborn, the ageless, the deathless, and the unconditioned. Nirvana can be compared to the clear blue sky that is always present even though it is often obscured by clouds. And when we clear away the obscurities brought about by the defilements of ignorance and craving, we experience the purity of mind that is, and always has been, present.

True and lasting happiness—the end of suffering—is not something that can be obtained through acquisition, rather it is *realized* through relinquishment and the extinction of the fires of greed, hatred, and delusion.

Section 3

The Noble Eightfold Path

The Fourth Noble Truth
Page 30

The Noble Eightfold Path

The Noble Eightfold Path is the Buddha's prescription for awakening, for the realization of true happiness. Unlike a physical path with a definite beginning, points of interest along the way, and finally the destination, this path has no beginning except a desire for lasting happiness followed by a gradual awakening to the true nature of Reality.

The path is divided into three groups or aspects: **Wisdom** (Right View, Right Intention), **Morality** (Right Speech, Right Action, Right Livelihood), and **Concentration** (Right Effort, Right Mindfulness, Right Concentration). Although there is a definite sequential progression from Right View to Right Concentration, these aspects and their components are interrelated. The components wind back on themselves again and again, much like switchbacks on a steep mountain trail. One who treads the way with persistence and dedication will find with each winding ever more subtle facets of the teachings.

The purpose of the Noble Eightfold Path is to undermine all the harmful mental and physical habit patterns one has developed over a lifetime. These patterns are built on wrong views—on a faulty understanding of the way things are. Wrong views lead to unskillful action. To overcome wrong views and unskillful action, one practices and applies the aspects of the path with persistent dedication.

Traditionally, the Wisdom aspect is presented first. Yet, a spiritual life cannot exist without at least trying to practice a virtuous life.

Wisdom Aspect
Morality Aspect
Concentration Aspect

Page 37
Wisdom

Page 38
Morality

Page 39
Concentration

The Eightfold Path
Page 36

Wisdom Aspect

Wisdom *(pañña)* is ultimately a profound understanding of the nature of reality, seeing with the mind's eye the truth of how things really are. Conventionally, it is the intelligent application of insight gained from experience. Our entire existence is a sequence of experiences, but experience alone does not create wisdom. Wisdom arises from within the stillness of a peaceful mind. It is stimulated by reflection on our actions and careful discernment of what each experience has to teach us. Wisdom arises from insight into the universal characteristics of impermanence, suffering, and not-self, and it leads to complete purification and liberation of the heart.

We are conditioned to see things a certain way, and we call that way reality. What we see (indeed, what we perceive through all of our senses) is colored with emotion and opinion and expectation. When circumstances—whether internal or external—change, our perceived reality changes along with them. True Reality stands apart from the unawakened person's perception of it.

The depth of one's wisdom relies upon the depth of one's concentration, which is the third aspect of the path.

The Wisdom aspect of the path begins with the cultivation of Right View. When one's view is correct, delusion is dispelled. Right Intention follows.

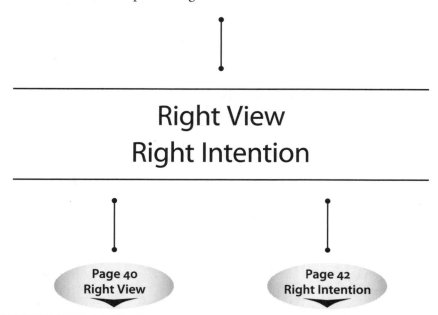

Right View
Right Intention

Page 40
Right View

Page 42
Right Intention

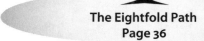

The Eightfold Path
Page 36

Morality Aspect

Virtue *(sila)* is the foundation on which the path aspects of Wisdom and Concentration are built. Leading a virtuous life brings the practice of the Middle Way into the world. A Buddhist does not lead a virtuous life because of a set of laws that must be obeyed with everlasting punishment the price of disobedience. Rather, a Buddhist practices morality because of a deep understanding that to do otherwise would bring an endless cycle of affliction to oneself and others.

Living a virtuous life is the outcome of understanding, which shapes our intentions, which manifest themselves as actions. The three components of the Morality aspect are Right Speech, Right Action, and Right Livelihood.

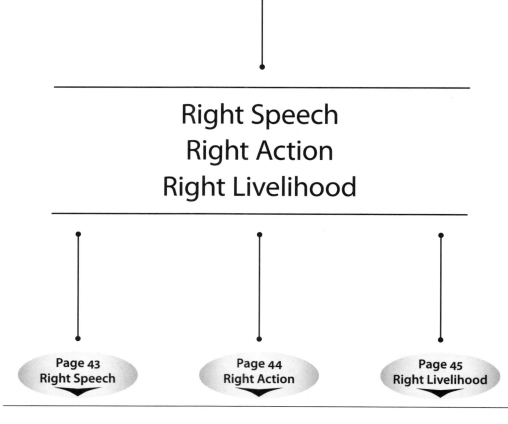

Right Speech
Right Action
Right Livelihood

Page 43
Right Speech

Page 44
Right Action

Page 45
Right Livelihood

The Eightfold Path
Page 36

Concentration Aspect

Concentration *(samadhi)* is the meditative—or mental development—aspect of the Middle Way. We can practice mental development throughout the day in every activity. Meditation doesn't necessarily mean sitting cross-legged on the floor. Four postures are mentioned in the scriptures as appropriate for meditation practice: standing, sitting, walking, and lying down. Regardless of the posture, it is through the stillness and focus of meditation that insights into the true nature of reality arise.

Right Effort and Right Mindfulness are necessary for each moment of Dharma practice. Right Mindfulness is a constant awareness of one's mental state and behavior; Right Effort brings about a wise response to those mental states and behaviors. Together they work with the other path factors to restrain what is not beneficial and cultivate what is beneficial, paving the way for deep peace, which is Right Concentration. Right Concentration is defined as the meditative absorptions *(jhanas)* and is often, but not necessarily, the first step before liberating Insight.

Right Effort
Right Mindfulness
Right Concentration

Page 46
Rigth Effort

Page 47
Right Mindfulness

Page 48
Right Concentration

Wisdom Aspect of the Eightfold Path
Page 37

Right View

There are many ways to view a thing, whether it is a molecule or the universe. Our view of things—how we see and interpret things around us—shapes our understanding of life itself. Right View is also known as Right Understanding. The Buddha presents Right View first because it is our view, our understanding of the world and how it works, that shapes our thoughts (the next step on the path) and, in turn, our actions (the steps that follow).

The Buddha teaches that there is a right way—and conversely a wrong way—to view and understand the Dharma. For some, this right/wrong dichotomy is an obstacle to Buddhism with its implication of judgment. This in itself comes from faulty understanding. ➤

Generosity

Virtue

Renunciation

Karma

The Four Noble Truths

Page 72
Right View

Wisdom Aspect of the Eightfold Path
Continued

Right View

If the goal is to build a house that will withstand severe weather, one wouldn't build it out of straw on a foundation of sand. To do so would be considered the wrong way to build. The right way to build a solid, durable house is not only by using sturdy materials, but also by using plans based on an understanding of materials and environmental conditions.

Right View is the solid and unshakable foundation on which all other aspects of the path are built. Developing Right View takes time and determination, with a gradual accumulation of understanding and insight as the fruit.

The Three Characteristics of Existence
The Five Aggregates
Rebirth and the Planes of Existence
Dependent Origination

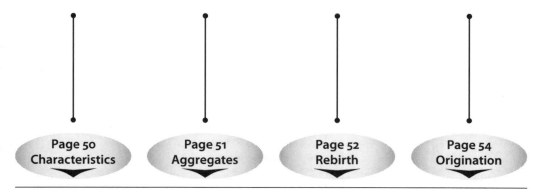

Page 50 Characteristics

Page 51 Aggregates

Page 52 Rebirth

Page 54 Origination

Wisdom Aspect of the Eightfold Path
Page 37

Right Intention

Right Intention is also called Right Thought or Right Resolve. Our view—how we understand and see the world—shapes our thoughts and intentions. In turn, thoughts and intentions shape our actions. For example, if we view the world as ripe for acquisition, then all our thoughts and intentions will be focused on acquiring wealth and power. We then act accordingly regardless of the consequences.

With intentions based on Right View, we can steer our actions in a wholesome direction. When we practice with Right Intention, we attempt to protect ourselves from thoughts that are harmful to us and to others. Three intentions are paramount in Buddhism.

Intention Toward Renunciation

Intention Toward Good Will

Intention Toward Harmlessness

Page 80
Right Intention

Morality Aspect of the Eightfold Path
Page 38

Right Speech

Words radiate power. Packed within them are the potential for benefit and the potential for harm. They can be used to build up or tear down, heal or wound, create safety or chaos.

The Buddha encourages us away from the four negative uses of words. Any form of lying—misrepresenting the truth in any way—creates mistrust. Divisive speech, that is, speech intended to pull people apart, creates disharmony. Words spoken with the intent to harm others is abusive and therefore creates ill feelings. Finally, idle chatter—talking just for the sake of talking—is considered of little value and should be avoided.

A skillful Buddhist's words are truthful, reliable, and dependable. They are harmonious and encouraging. One who practices Right Speech uses words that are pleasant to hear, heartfelt, and courteous. And finally, one uses words that are meaningful, to the point, reasonable, and timely. Timeliness is important because there are occasions when speaking truthfully or meaningfully could cause a negative response. Such words spoken at the wrong time, however pleasantly, could do unintended damage.

As a factor of the Noble Eightfold Path, Right Speech is truthful, harmonious, pleasant and meaningful.

Truthful

Harmonious

Pleasant

Meaningful

Morality Aspect of the Eightfold Path
Page 38

Right Action

From the beginning, the Buddha points out that suffering and pain for us and for others are caused by desire. Within the untrained mind, desire leads directly to the actions that will fulfill it. We are gripped by the delusion that the fulfillment of desire will bring happiness.

When we abandon certain negative actions and cultivate certain positive actions, we can eliminate desire and foster peace and contentment within ourselves as well as influence those qualities in others. Negative actions are explained in the Five Precepts. Positive actions include the practice of Generosity (Right View) and the cultivation of the Four Sublime Abidings (Right Mindfulness) and the Ten Perfections.

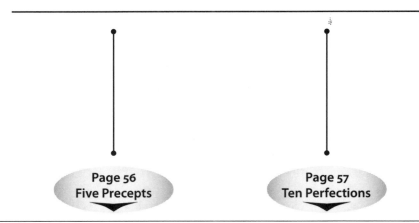

The Five Precepts
The Ten Perfections

Page 56
Five Precepts

Page 57
Ten Perfections

Morality Aspect of the Eightfold Path
Page 38

Right Livelihood

Livelihood is the means of obtaining the necessities of life. It is how we maintain ourselves in the world and is an integral part of our existence. For the monastic sangha, Right Livelihood means keeping some 227 precepts, including relying on alms for food, robes, and other necessities. The Buddha forbade monks and nuns from having or using money.

The Buddha had fewer expectations of the lay community, because he understood that a life of renunciation was not for everyone, even for those who aspired to higher spiritual practices. Therefore, a livelihood that is considered right is one based on sound moral principles. Certain occupations, however, are not conducive to spiritual practice because they cause us to breach those principles and thus cause harm to ourselves and others. In the day of the Buddha, five occupations were considered wrong livelihood: trading in weapons, human beings, meat, intoxicants, and poisons.

In our world of entangled global commerce, in which we have no control over how money is made and who is harmed, in which socioeconomic status both dictates and limits our options, participating in a right livelihood is often a challenge. Yet, we can strive to minimize any direct harm we do by steering our intentions in the direction of what is good. We can take responsibility for *all* our actions, even those that may seem to be out of our control.

Concentration Aspect of the Eightfold Path
Page 39

Right Effort

To accomplish anything worthwhile, we must put effort into the task, no matter what the task is. With effort we can abandon thoughts, views, and intentions that are unskillful, that is, qualities that lead to affliction of ourselves and others. And with effort we can cultivate thoughts, views, and intentions that are skillful, that bring benefit to ourselves and to others.

A synonym for *effort* is "energy." Without energy there is no effort. Sometimes, with all the challenges of life bearing down on us, it seems easier just to do nothing. Even the smallest bit of energy seems impossible to muster. But nothing is accomplished without effort or energy. Without energy, boredom sets in and vitality is replaced by lethargy.

Boredom is a form of suffering. Understanding and overcoming suffering is why the Buddha left his family and his palace. To understand and overcome suffering takes energy.

It is with effort that we strive to comprehend the Wisdom aspect, practice the Morality aspect, and apply the Concentration aspect of the Middle Way. Only with persistent effort can greed, hatred, and delusion be overcome and replaced by true and lasting happiness. The Buddha's prescription for overcoming suffering includes the Four Great Efforts.

The Four Great Efforts

Page 84
Four Great Efforts

Concentration Aspect of the Eightfold Path
Page 39

Right Mindfulness

Mindfulness has two meanings. In one sense it is the quality of being aware of what is happening in the present moment. With keen observation of the mind, we can see how we spend most of our time lost in either the past or the future. Thoughts of past or future events churn constantly. If we are paying attention at all, we see that rarely are we satisfied with what is happening right now. But with mindfulness we can focus a spotlight on the present.

The second meaning of mindfulness is "remembering." With mindfulness we remember where we are—in the here and now—and the importance of being there. We remember to make the Four Great Efforts and to keep the Five Precepts.

It isn't enough, however, merely to see what is happening right now. Clear comprehension is the quality of discernment, the ability to understand fully what is happening in the light of wisdom. On the deepest level, what is happening is the rising and passing away of phenomena. With mindfulness we remember the instructions to focus on what is happening without interpretation, without delusion.

The Four Foundations of Mindfulness
The Six Sense Bases and their Objects
The Seven Factors for Awakening
Insight into the Four Noble Truths

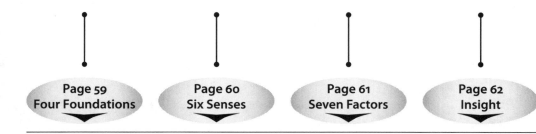

Page 59
Four Foundations

Page 60
Six Senses

Page 61
Seven Factors

Page 62
Insight

Concentration Aspect of the Eightfold Path
Page 39

Right Concentration

Concentration (samadhi) is a one-pointedness of mind. In meditation we bring our attention to a single object—usually the breath. The mind remains focused there, serving as a benchmark for the mental phenomena that come and go. We observe the phenomena but are not caught up in them.

Synonymous with Right Concentration is *jhana*—meditative absorption—of which there are several levels. Its purpose is to rid the mind of the influences of the negative mental states called the Five Hindrances so that deeper wisdom (insights) can be realized.

Buddhist meditation has two components of mental development, tranquility *(samatha)* and insight *(vipassana)*. Although they have different functions in our practice, these elements work together and reinforce each other. Both are necessary and are not different paths or practices. With tranquility (the cause), one forms the conditions for insight (the effect).

Right Concentration offers us real peace, clarity, and contentment, and thus, we can dwell in the *Brahma Viharas*, or Sublime Abidings.

The Five Hindrances
The Sublime Abidings
Tranquility and the Jhanas

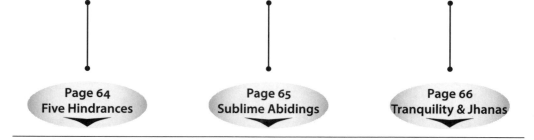

Page 64
Five Hindrances

Page 65
Sublime Abidings

Page 66
Tranquility & Jhanas

Section 4

The Factors of the Path in Detail

Right View
Page 41

The Three Characteristics of Existence

All things in existence are brought about—or arise—as a result of an infinite chain of causes and conditions. All conditioned things are endowed with three characteristics: They are impermanent *(anicca),* unsatisfactory *(dukkha),* and not-self *(anatta).* Because of these characteristics, nothing that arises through causes and conditions can bring true happiness. Therefore, no conditioned thing—whether an idea, a person, a house, or a nation—can be a true and lasting refuge.

In Buddhism, only Nirvana is unconditioned; that is, there is no cause or set of conditions that brings it into existence. It simply is.

Impermanence

Unsatisfactoriness

Not-self

Page 71
Characteristics

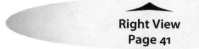

Right View
Page 41

The Five Aggregates

An aggregate is a mass or heap of things whose constituent parts retain their own characteristics. The Buddha spoke of living beings being a conglomerate of five main groups, or aggregates. Physical matter belongs to the aggregate of body, including not just human and animal bodies, but the more subtle bodies of beings in other realms.

Mental objects fall into one of four aggregates, which together are called mind. The four aggregates of mind are feelings, perceptions, mental formations, and consciousness.

Human beings, then, are composed of the five aggregates of mind and body.

In Pali, mind and body is stated as *nama-rupa,* which has long been rendered as "name-and-form." A more contemporary rendering is "mentality and materiality."

Body

Feelings

Perceptions

Mental Formations

Consciousness

Page 74
Aggregates

Right View
Page 41

Rebirth and the Planes of Existence

The Buddhist doctrine of rebirth is not the same as the Hindu doctrine of reincarnation. In reincarnation, a personal and unchangeable essence is born into a certain—and inescapable—caste according to the actions of a previous life. In Buddhism, however, there is no unchangeable being or essence of being that travels from one lifetime to the next.

In rebirth there is nothing personal, no "thing" or essence that transmigrates from one body to another. Instead, one's actions in this lifetime create the conditions for rebirth.

Rebirth is the natural outcome in the cycle of cause and effect called samsara, the wheel of life. At the moment of death, one's stream of consciousness will be affected by karma from habitual past behavior—the powerful positive and negative actions one has done—and by one's mental state as death nears. Rebirth is a direct result of clinging to life. It is how the law of karma, the law of cause and effect, plays out through the vast expanses of time.

Rebirth does not necessarily occur in the human realm. In all, according to the Pali Cannon, there are 31 planes of existence encompassed in three different realms. From lowest to highest we find the Sensual Realm (11 planes, also called the Desire Realm), the Fine-material Realm (16 planes occupied by devas, also called the Form Realm), and the Immaterial Realm (4 planes, also occupied by devas and sometimes referred to as the Formless Realm). ➤

Sensual Realm
Fine-material Realm
Immaterial Realm

Page 53
Planes of Existence

**Right View
Continued**

Rebirth and the Planes of Existence

Rebirth can be into any plane, depending on the accumulation of karma. A being could spend eons of time in one plane, yet there is always the possibility for a higher, or lower, rebirth. Unlike the Judeo-Christian concepts of eternal damnation in hell or eternal salvation in heaven, none of the Buddhist realms are places of permanent dwelling. Because all conditioned things are impermanent, even these worlds come into and out of existence, as do the beings in them. Only Nirvana is unconditioned and unchanging.

The planes of the Fine-material Realm can be attained through the four lower meditative absorptions, or *jhanas* (pp. 66, 94).

Beings in the Immaterial Realm have no body, only mind. They are unable to hear the Dharma. It is possible for practiced meditators to access the Immaterial Realm through the Immaterial Attainments (p. 94).

Discussed below are the beings of the Sensual Realm.

Devas

Humans

Asuras

Animals

Pretas

Hell Beings

**Page 76
Sensual Realm**

**Right View
Page 41**

Dependent Origination

Dependent Origination is a teaching the Buddha gave to explain how living beings are born, exist, die, and are reborn, all without an undying self or soul.

Closely related to Dependent Origination is the Law of Conditionality. It explains how all things that come into being—whether it be a human life, a thought, or a galaxy—depend upon an endless chain of preceding causes and conditions. This law also is a way of looking at the second and third Noble Truths. The second truth—there is a cause of suffering—can be stated as, *Because of this, there is that.* The third truth—there is an end of suffering— can be stated as, *Without this, that cannot be.* Remove the causes and conditions of a given "thing," and that thing cannot come to be. Remove the causes and conditions of suffering, and suffering ceases.

With the 12 Links of Dependent Origination, the Buddha provides a model of the causal chain that binds an individual to samsara, the endless cycle of suffering.

The 12 Links of Dependent Origination

**Page 55
Twelve Links**

Right View
Page 54

The 12 Links of Dependent Origination

The 12 Links of Dependent Origination—also called the Wheel of Life—illustrates how the unenlightened person remains in samsara, the cycle of endless suffering from one rebirth to the next.

The first two links, Ignorance and Volition, can be understood as a past lifetime. The last two links of Rebirth followed by Old Age and Death can be understood as a future lifetime. The eight links in between are considered a present lifetime. These lifetimes are separate in a generic sense, yet each is causally linked.

Ignorance	Consciousness	Rebirth
Volition	Mind & Body	Old Age & Death
	The Six Senses	
	Contact	
	Feelings	
	Craving	
	Clinging	
	Existence	

Page 78
Twelve Links

**Right Action
Page 44**

The Five Precepts

The Five Precepts are presented in the form of basic rules of training. They involve five categories of action one should abstain from. The precepts are not commandments in the traditional religious sense of the word. There is no judge, and no punishment (other than perhaps civil) will befall those who break them. On the contrary, the precepts are freely chosen standards to live by out of compassion for oneself and for all beings. As such, they help the practitioner avoid making bad karma.

When we observe the precepts, we offer others absolute safety.

Abstaining from Killing

Abstaining from Taking Things Not Given

Abstaining from Sexual Misconduct

Abstaining from Lying

Abstaining from Intoxicants

**Page 81
Precepts**

**Right Action
Page 44**

The Ten Perfections

Although the Buddha spoke about all the qualities of the Ten Perfections, a specific list didn't come together until well after the his death. The qualities were recognized as what an aspirant to buddhahood—a bodhisattva—would need to perfect in order to become a fully self-awakened buddha. As Buddhism grew as a religion, the Jataka stories evolved as tales ascribed to the Bodhisattva Gautama during his many past existences. Each tale is an exemplar of one or more of these qualities.

In every case, the Ten Perfections are directed toward all beings out of deep compassion, with the wish that they be free from all forms of suffering and attain only the highest levels of rebirth.

Generosity	**Patience**
Virtue	**Truthfulness**
Renunciation	**Resolution**
Wisdom	**Loving Kindness**
Energy	**Equanimity**

**Page 82
Perfections**

**Right Effort
Page 46**

The Four Great Efforts

Nothing of value can be attained without effort. The Four Great Efforts are applied directly to the mind, where skillful qualities can be developed.

With effort we can recognize and avoid unskillful thoughts at the moment of their inception, and we can overcome unskillful thoughts already there. Also, with effort we can recognize skillful thoughts as they arise, then develop and maintain them.

Effort to Avoid

Effort to Overcome

Effort to Develop

Effort to Maintain

Page 84
Four Great Efforts

Right Mindfulness
Page 47

The Four Foundations of Mindfulness

Mindfulness is that special quality of being aware of what is happening right now. A moment of mindfulness will underscore how much we relive the past and fret about the future but ignore the present. Remorseful or angry thoughts about what happened yesterday compete with worrisome or expectant thoughts about what may happen tomorrow. These thoughts tend to repeat themselves in an infinite loop. The present goes by without notice.

The practice of mindfulness begins with putting aside all our worldly concerns—all grasping, grief, and worry. We apply the first two Great Efforts to quell any disruptive thoughts that arise or have already arisen. Then we focus on one of the Four Foundations of Mindfulness, also called as the Four Frames of Reference.

Mindfulness of the Body

Mindfulness of Feelings

Mindfulness of the Mind

Mindfulness of Mental Objects

Page 86
Four Foundations

Right Mindfulness
Page 47

The Six Senses and Their Objects

Without form—that is, the body—the senses cannot exist. Objects of the senses—things we see and touch, for example—also belong to the aggregate of form. When one of the senses comes into contact with an object, feeling spontaneously arises followed quickly by perception, so long as consciousness is present at the moment of contact.

Buddhism introduces a sixth sense beyond the usual five: the mind.

In Buddhism the senses are sometimes referred to as sense doors, that is, the doors through which perceptions enter.

The Eye and Visible Objects

The Ear and Sounds

The Nose and Scents

The Tongue and Tastes

The Body and Tactile Objects

The Mind and Thoughts

Right Mindfulness
Page 47

The Seven Factors for Awakening

Full development and mastery of the Seven Factors for Awakening is necessary for awakening, and developing them leads inexorably to awakening and liberation. Any of them can be cultivated as an object of meditation; during meditation it can be refined and made stronger and stronger. When the Seven Factors are mastered they become part of the mental continuum, the stream of consciousness that runs throughout the day.

Mindfulness

Investigation of the Dharma

Energy

Rapture

Tranquility

Concentration

Equanimity

Page 90
Seven Factors

Right Mindfulness
Page 47

Insight into the Four Noble Truths

Initially we must have a basic understanding of the Four Noble Truths. Insight, however, requires more that mere familiarity with them. Insight requires that we develop the skills to see how they apply directly to each of us. To gain insight, we first identify an aspect of our lives that may be actually or potentially troublesome. We then focus on it in order to comprehend it as suffering, as prescribed under the First Noble Truth. Next, through honest discernment we identify the cause and see that the cause must be eradicated (Second Noble Truth) to realize the end of suffering (Third Noble Truth). And, finally, we apply the Fourth Noble Truth by developing the specific path factors we know will bring suffering to an end.

Insight is a deep understanding of the true nature of things both mental and physical. During meditation, after the mind is concentrated and calm, we can examine what arises and see that all phenomena are impermanent, unsatisfactory, and without any real and enduring substance.

Insight answers the question, "What happens when I cling to as my own that which is impermanent, unsatisfactory, and insubstantial?" The answer is, "Suffering happens, pain happens." These are the First and Second Noble Truths: suffering and its cause.

During meditation this insight becomes experience, and we see that there is a way to bring an end to suffering, the Third Noble Truth. We learn from experience that clinging is detrimental to our health and well-being. We learn, by following the Noble Eightfold Path, how we can gradually improve our health and well-being by loosening the grip on all those ideas that we once believed defined us and supported us.

Insight gives us the courage to ask, "What happens when I release all of my firmly held beliefs in how things are and how they should be?" and gives us the courage to hear the quiet and possibly alarming answer, which is the experience of insight itself: "This human condition is merely a flow of events without a 'me' whatsoever."

Arriving at this solution is more difficult than it seems because our ego insists that we are permanent, that we can create satisfaction for ourselves, and that we have a unique core substance that makes us who we are. Our psyche insists we are special because we are different from all others.

With insight we recognize we are not what we thought we were. Rather, each of us is an ever-changing process, with each part of that process arising and passing away just as each breath arises and passes away. We see there is nothing that can be clung to, just as the breath cannot be clung to. ➤

**Right Mindfulness
Continued**

Insight into the Four Noble Truths

With insight our view of the world becomes clear. We are able to distinguish what is true from what is false, what is valuable from what is worthless because we have put aside all doubts as to the Buddha, Dharma, and Sangha.

Confusion and uncertainty are replaced by clarity of vision. We understand that our actions are not nearly so important as what's in our hearts. We no longer perform "good" actions just for the good results they will bring. Rather, wisdom leads to a purity of intention, speech, and action that manifests outwardly as a natural morality and inwardly as an empty flow of phenomena.

Insight happens when all the factors of the Noble Eightfold Path are developed and in balance. Right View, the first factor of the path, has become the foundation of our behavior. With insight we realize the Unconditioned, the Deathless, Nirvana.

Suffering
The Cause of Suffering
The End of Suffering
The Way to the End of Suffering

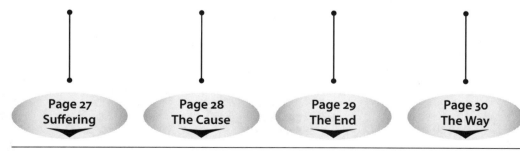

**Page 27
Suffering**

**Page 28
The Cause**

**Page 29
The End**

**Page 30
The Way**

Right Concentration
Page 48

The Five Hindrances

The Five Hindrances are obstacles to meditation, to happiness, and to leading a satisfying life in general. Dealing with the hindrances during meditation is to come to know and understand their power and to develop the skills to overcome them instead of being governed by them. The Buddha uses the simile of a pot of water in which one with good vision can see a clear and true reflection of oneself—so long as the water is clean and undisturbed. Each of the hindrances has a corresponding metaphorical impediment to clarity.

Recognizing and responding to the Five Hindrances during meditation is practice for dealing with them during everyday life.

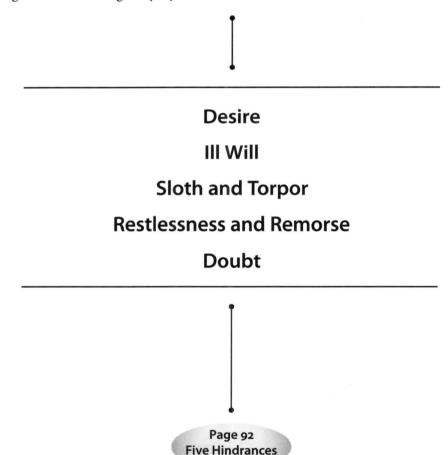

Desire

Ill Will

Sloth and Torpor

Restlessness and Remorse

Doubt

Page 92
Five Hindrances

Right Concentration
Page 48

The Four Sublime Abidings

The Sublime Abidings are also called the Brahma Viharas, the Divine Abodes, and the Immeasurable Minds.

The practice of the Sublime Abidings is done with the understanding that we are no different from one another in our longing to be happy and free from suffering. Initially, we strive to develop these qualities within our own hearts. Then we gradually reach out to those who are near to us, pervading them with kindness and compassion and appreciating their good qualities while understanding and accepting their unpleasant ones.

Eventually, we are able to permeate the entire world with these qualities and include in our best wishes all beings, even those who do not share our views or intend us harm.

Loving Kindness

Compassion

Appreciation

Equanimity

Page 93
Sublime Abidings

Right Concentration
Page 48

Tranquility and the Jhanas

Tranquility, or serenity, arises when our attention is maintained on one thing, perception, or process—the breath, for example—for extended periods. This concentration brings the object of meditation, whatever it may be, into focus. When the mind wanders and is disturbed by one or more of the Five Hindrances (p. 64), we use mindfulness to notice the wandering and then make the effort to bring the mind back to the object, maintaining it there. Becoming more deeply absorbed in the meditation induces states of tranquility.

When we develop tranquility, desire, aversion, and doubt are dispelled. When the mind is serene, insights into the true nature of existence can arise. We begin to see things as they truly are.

With insight comes wisdom. With wisdom, ignorance is overcome. Wisdom leads to Nirvana.

When the mind is fully concentrated on the object of meditation, we enter a state of absorption called *jhana* in Pali and *dhyana* in Sanskrit. There are eight levels of meditative absorption, but, like all conditioned things, they are temporary. Practiced meditators, however, can enter them with ease and remain in them for long periods. The fourth absorption is the staging area from which one can develop much loftier spiritual powers that arise in the fifth through eighth absorptions.

In jhana one unifies with the object of meditation, and the five senses temporarily stop functioning. The result is a very pure and powerful state of joy and clarity. This clarity leads to deep Insight.

We should understand, however, that these states—even the attainment of the highest level of absorption—are not the goal. Before the Buddha's awakening he was a master meditator, as were many of his contemporaries. The goal is the understanding and application of the Four Noble Truths: Wisdom.

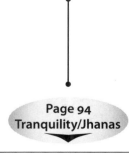

Page 94
Tranquility/Jhanas

Section 5

Further Definitions

The First Noble Truth
Page 27

The Three Kinds of Suffering

Ordinary Suffering

Ordinary suffering includes the everyday stresses such as birth, grief, despair, pain, sickness, old age, and death. Also within this category is the suffering of not being with those we wish to be with, being with those we wish not to be with, not getting what we want, getting what we don't want, being in situations we don't want to be in, and not being in those we do. Ordinary suffering is common to everyone and therefore is something that is easily understood on an experiential level.

Suffering of Change

The Buddha teaches that all things are impermanent. Everything changes. When things change, when conditions change—even in the smallest degree—suffering arises. The suffering of change is not necessarily painful in the everyday sense of ordinary suffering. But because everything is in a constant state of flux, nothing has the ability to fully satisfy. This is dukkha, and it leaves us vaguely uncomfortable.

Suffering of change is not easily recognized while it occurs. Change happens so often and so fast that we adjust and adapt automatically without noticing what is happening. We cope in whatever ways we can. So often, however, many of these ways lead to yet more pain and suffering, even if we don't realize the sequence as it is happening.

The practice of Buddhism is a study of subtleties. At what point does something subtle and unnoticeable become obvious and palpable? At what point do we *comprehend* suffering? The more we practice, the more we see that every change has the potential to give rise to stress and suffering.

Suffering of Conditioned Existence

We live in a world of conditions that change moment to moment. What we consider the "self" is an aggregation of ever-changing causes and conditions. The Five Aggregates (p. 51) are the physical and mental components of a being. The body, for example, comes into existence through a series of causes and conditions, without which there would be no body at all. Throughout life, the body relies on conditions to keep it alive.

These conditions, however, are ever changing. So too the body is changing from one moment to the next. Suffering is when we cling to and identify with any element of the body and mind. In brief, grasping after the Five Aggregates is, by its very nature, dukkha.

The Second Noble Truth
Page 31

Craving

Craving for Sensual Pleasure

Sensual pleasures includes pleasurable tactile experiences, tastes, sounds, sights, smells, and thoughts. Desire for sensually pleasurable experiences lays a foundation for suffering because only short-term satisfaction can come from them. When the experience passes, dissatisfaction arises and once again we set out on yet another endless-cycle quest for satisfaction.

Aversion to or avoidance of the unpleasant is craving to be *rid* of unpleasant experiences. Fear and anger are forms of aversion that burrow deep into our subconscious where they become powerful catalysts for action. Wanting what we don't have, wanting to be with those we love but who are apart from us, getting what we don't want, and being with people we don't like also give rise to pain and suffering.

Craving for accomplishment, recognition, or status can be an immediate or a latent source of suffering: immediate when in every moment these lofty goals are not reached and latent when they fail to satisfy or there is the inevitable fall from grace. Wanting things to be prettier, better, faster—indeed, any form of craving—is dissatisfaction with how things are in this moment. We are insisting on change; we are assuming we can control both the change and the outcome.

Craving for Existence

The craving for existence is the will to *be*, to survive even if survival is unpleasant. Craving for existence is not wrong in the conventional sense of the word. However, because beings with this craving are bound with a sense of self that must be protected and preserved, the result is dukkha.

Craving for Nonexistence

Craving for nonexistence is a will directed toward annihilation (suicide for example) or a desire not be reborn. This craving leads to suffering and endless karmic repercussions.

The Second Noble Truth
Page 33

The Three Fires

Greed

Any aspect of wanting, regardless of its intensity, falls into the category of greed. The exception, as noted previously, is dhamma-chanda, the aspiration to, or desire for, awakening and thereby total release from the infinite cycle of suffering.

On a subtle level, any seeking of pleasure through the senses is part of what is meant by greed—a difficult concept to digest because of our conditioning to seek pleasure. Pleasure, we are told, is good and desirable. And, just as a plant's roots seek water, beings naturally are attracted to anything that is pleasurable.

It's not so difficult to see how extreme greed will lead to suffering, but what about the subtler forms? How, for example, could listening to good music be considered detrimental? Recall that all conditioned things, music included, are impermanent, unsatisfactory, and without an enduring substance. Even when we find the music enthralling and satisfying in the moment, it will eventually end. Then we will grasp at something else—more music, perhaps—to fill the void of dissatisfaction. The problem is not the music so much as it is the attachment to it.

When wanting leads to clinging—holding on to and protecting what we've acquired—and struggling to make permanent that which is impermanent, suffering is the inevitable result.

Hatred

Hatred is the opposite of greed and comprises all aspects of aversion. It is the pushing away of discomfort and pain and, like greed, has many levels.

It is natural to avoid anything painful or uncomfortable, even on the subtlest of levels. However, hatred and aversion are in themselves forms of suffering. We cannot escape unpleasant circumstances, but we can change our view of them and how we respond to them.

Delusion

We are under the delusion that we as individuals are something greater than an aggregation of ever-changing phenomena. Delusion extends to all things we hold dear. Yet nothing, except Nirvana, is permanent and enduring.

We are also under the delusion that happiness is a commodity that can be acquired like a new car or a new relationship. *If only things would be this way,* or *if I had _____, then I would be happy.* True happiness cannot be found outside of oneself. It is always within. We fail to see this, however, because the function of delusion is to keep us in the dark.

Right View
Page 50

The Three Characteristics of Existence

Impermanence

All conditioned things are impermanent. Anything that comes into existence, therefore, must eventually go out of existence.

Within the human body, millions of cells come into and go out of existence each minute, yet there is an appearance of continuity. Even things that are seemingly permanent—a mountain, the ocean, the earth, the universe—are changing, sometimes in subtle, imperceptible ways and other times in grand and obvious ways.

Any change, regardless of how small, signifies the end of one thing and the beginning of another.

Unsatisfactoriness

Because of their impermanent nature, all conditioned things are, eventually, unsatisfactory, even things we consider good and satisfying in the moment. These, too, become unsatisfactory over time because they break, run away, die, or lose their hold on our interest. What brings us happiness and joy today will—in some small or huge way—likely bring us sorrow and suffering tomorrow.

Not-self

A conditioned thing, being ever-changing, is insubstantial: It has no unchanging essence or self. This is as true for human beings as it is for any other object in the universe.

The doctrine of not-self does not mean that individual people or things don't exist. When we refer to ourselves, we certainly mean things that are distinct, concrete, and in existence, albeit an ever changing flow of existence.

From a Buddhist perspective, however, there is nothing about a person that can be pinned down as self. The body is not-self; it is not ultimately who or what we are. This holds true for the other of the five aggregates of feelings, perceptions, mental formations, and consciousness.

Right View
Page 40

Right View

Generosity

A lack of generosity makes spiritual progress difficult. Clinging to what we have sets up artificial boundaries between ourselves and others and reinforces the sense of self, which separates rather than unites.

Generosity does not mean if you get more, I get less. Instead, it is the notion that there is enough to go around. It allows us to let go of the conventional ways of viewing the world.

Generosity puts us into accord with others, even if it is not appreciated. Generosity for its own sake brings a happiness that doesn't tarnish like the happiness based on greed, hatred, and delusion. One who practices generosity does so without expectations of return. The purpose is in the act of giving itself.

Generosity is the first component of Right View because it is the easiest to begin practicing. For instance, we can start small with giving freely of our good will. Thus a foundation is laid for the greater forms of virtue.

Virtue

With generosity as a beginning, we can continue to develop the qualities that make us agreeable to others. Living a virtuous life means living a blameless life, a life lived in such a way that does not give others—or ourselves—cause for criticism or concern.

With Right View we see how a blameless life leads to a calm mind, a mind in which insights can arise.

Renunciation

Renunciation is similar to generosity, but it has no object, no "other" involved. An act of renunciation is one of letting go, not only of material things we don't really need as a means of simplifying our lives, but also of ideas. One of the hardest things to let go of is our view of how things "should" be. The grip we have on our view of self and others must be loosened before we can begin to see the true nature of reality. ➤

Right View
Continued

Right View

Karma

Karma is often misunderstood as fate or as a kind of payback for bad behavior. Karma, however, is action with intention, not the result of an action. And there is intention—good or bad—in nearly everything we do. Typically, we ignore, are unaware of, or are deluded about the intentions behind our actions.

The Buddha teaches that wholesome actions bring good results and unwholesome actions bring bad results. Often the results are not immediately seen or understood, but they are there—or will be there—although they have nothing to do with judgment, punishment, or reward.

Sometimes it seems unavoidable that suffering arises from our actions, even those done with the best of intention. But intention as well as other circumstances do indeed mitigate the karmic consequences of our actions.

When we reflect on the results of karma, we must differentiate between our own actions and the actions of others. For example, **Person A's** actions (**A's** karma, which is based solely on the degree of greed, hatred, and delusion present) do not cause **Person B's** actions. Rather **B** reacts to **A** according to **B's** own level of greed, hatred, and delusion. These reactions become **B's** karma.

What we do yields both immediate and future results. We cannot change the past, but we can affect the future through a careful and considered choice of actions. This is what made the Buddha's teaching revolutionary in his time: It is our actions in the here and now, not the circumstances of our birth, that affect our present and our future.

The Four Noble Truths

The Buddha begins his teaching with the Four Noble Truths: there is suffering, there is a cause of suffering, an end of suffering is possible, and there is a specific means to the end of suffering.

The fourth truth is the Noble Eightfold Path. The first factor in the path is Right View, that is, the correct and thorough understanding of how things really are. It is essential, then, to cultivate a thorough understanding of the Four Noble Truths.

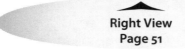

Right View
Page 51

The Five Aggregates

Body

Body is the form aspect of name-and-form, nama-rupa. Body refers not just to our own physical being, but to all physical objects. Only the sentient being (one who is able to perceive things), however, possesses the name—mind or mentality—aspect of name-and-form. Only the sentient being has feelings, perceptions, mental formations, and consciousness.

Feelings

What we usually think of as feelings—anger and love, for example—are really emotions and therefore fall into the aggregate of mental formations. The aggregate of feelings is reserved for three special aspects of the mind: pleasant, unpleasant, or neutral (neither pleasant nor unpleasant). With everything we sense through seeing, hearing, smelling, tasting, touching, and cognizing there arises an immediate reaction experienced as one of these three kinds of feelings, which will vary from person to person. Beauty, comfort, and deliciousness are examples of pleasant feelings. A grating sound, a bad smell, and a self-deprecating thought are examples of unpleasant feelings. A neutral feeling is one of indifference and does not arouse any response.

Perceptions

Perceptions are the labels we put on things as they arise within our consciousness. Perception is the recognition of phenomena. Like feelings, perceptions arise very quickly and usually without our realizing it. We form perceptions around the six senses and their objects: perceptions of forms (objects of sight), sounds, odors, tastes, touch, and mental objects.

If we see a bird, for example, immediately we label it *bird*. And, depending on our disposition toward that bird, a pleasant, unpleasant, or neutral feeling will arise at the moment of perception. ➤

The Five Aggregates

Mental Formations

A mental formation is will directed toward a perception that, as stated earlier, surrounds one of the six senses and its object. Will is the mental faculty by which one forms an intention. Volition is the faculty of using one's will to direct the mind toward that which is good, bad, or neutral.

For example, we see a disturbing picture or a story in the newspaper. We perceive the information. An unpleasant feeling arises; then anger arises. Anger is a mental formation. It is anger that stirs mental activity, that is, volition. At this point we can expect karmic effects. No karmic effects are produced by perceptions or feelings in and of themselves. It is only at the point of *mental* formation that such action is produced.

The aggregate of mental formations includes all the mind states that we customarily refer to as feelings, for example, happiness, sorrow, and fear as well as conceit, wisdom, energy, confidence, and concentration. Buddhist texts name 52 mental states.

The process of mental activity is instantaneous, ongoing, and always changing.

Consciousness

Consciousness is awareness that arises at one or more of the six sense doors. A sense door is a functioning sense organ: the eye, nose, ear, tongue, skin, and mind.

For consciousness to arise there must be a sense door (for example, the eye) and an object (something to see). When these factors come together, sense contact occurs. With sense contact, eye consciousness—awareness directed toward seeing—arises.

Without a sense door or an object, there can be no contact. Without contact, consciousness cannot arise. Without consciousness, nothing can exist in our awareness.

Right View
Page 53

The Sensual Realm

Devas

In the Sensual Realm are six planes of existence within the Heaven Realms. These realms are occupied by deities referred to in Buddhist literature as devas or radiant beings. A deva's existence is primarily happy, relatively free from suffering. Although devas are capable of practicing the Dharma (recall that it was a deva who encouraged the Buddha to begin teaching the Dharma after his discovery of the Four Noble Truths), there would seem to be no need to.

Yet, despite their refined nature, devas are subject to the same afflictions of sickness, old age, death, and delusion as are humans. Devas also are subject to boredom, complacency, and arrogance. Devas, too, are subject to rebirth depending on their karma—their actions through previous rebirths.

Humans

In Buddhism, to have rebirth in the Human Realm is more desirable than rebirth in even the highest of the Heaven Realms. That is why the Buddha himself took rebirth for the last time in the Human Realm, so that he could discover and then teach the true nature of reality and the end of suffering. To bring suffering to an end is to bring samsara to an end, the cycle of rebirth through eons of time in which beings are trapped.

Of all the 31 planes of existence, the Human Realm is best for Dharma practice. Within the Human Realm beings have a relative balance between happiness and misery. Therefore, when the desire to escape the wheel of suffering is powerful enough, humans have the opportunity to do so through Dharma practice.

Asuras

Asuras are powerful, bad-natured beings, aggressive and arrogant. Asuras, sometimes referred to as jealous gods or titans, are regularly at war with devas in the vain attempt to prove their superiority.

Animals

Driven by uncontrolled lust, inhabitants of the Animal Realm are beings who live solely for the constant gratification of their immediate and overpowering desires. These beings mainly live by instinct, without regard to the consequences of their actions. The Animal Realm is dominated by the desire to kill and the fear of being killed. Animals live within a dense cloud of delusion. ➤

Right View
Continued

The Sensual Realm

Pretas

Pretas, also called hungry ghosts, are never satisfied. Their suffering is based on living in a constant state of discontent. Theirs are lives of misery and torment because they can never get enough to fill the void that seems to grow bigger and bigger.

Pretas are often depicted as having tiny mouths and huge but empty bellies, impossible to fill.

Hell Beings

Hell is the place of unspeakable suffering and torment. It is the worst possible place imaginable, much like the Judeo-Christian hell.

The Buddhist Hell Realm, however, is significantly different. As terrible as it is, beings with a rebirth in Hell are there as a direct result of their actions (karma), not because they are being punished by an external entity after being judged as unworthy. Nor do beings in Hell—as well as in the other realms—dwell there for eternity. Even Hell beings have an opportunity for higher rebirth. Although it may take eons of time, a thousand eons is not the same as eternity.

Right View
Page 55

The 12 Links of Dependent Origination

Ignorance

Ignorance of the true nature of the way things are—that is, ignorance of the Four Noble Truths—is the reason why beings circle perpetually in the cycle of life known as samsara. It is also the first link in the chain of Dependent Origination.

Because of this fundamental ignorance, we do not understand that our suffering is the direct result of our volitional actions (karma). Ignorance, then, leads to volitional action.

Volition

Volition is willful action (karma formations), which is the direct result of ignorance. Through our actions we make things "come to be" out of ignorance. When ignorance is eradicated, there is no volition and the cycle is ended.

When ignorance and volition persist, however, the law of karma dictates that the results of our actions persist even beyond death. If upon death there is unresolved karma, energy, called relinking consciousness, springs forth. Volition, then, leads to consciousness.

Consciousness

The consciousness that forms a new rebirth is dependent upon the volition of the previous birth. Consciousness leads to the name-and-form (mind and body) of a new being.

Mind and Body

Mind and body—also referred to as name-and-form—are dependent on consciousness. A mind and a body then leads to the six senses.

The Six Senses

Without mind and body there cannot be the six senses of seeing, hearing, smelling, tasting, touching and cognizing. Senses lead to contact with their objects: sights, sounds, smells, tastes, tactile things, and thoughts.

Contact

Without the senses there can be no contact with their objects. When contact occurs, feelings arise.   ➤

Right View
Page 55

The 12 Links of Dependent Origination

Feelings

Feelings, which depend upon contact, are pleasant, unpleasant, or neutral. Feelings lead to craving in the form of desire, aversion, or indifference.

Craving

Craving is dependent upon feelings. Based on feelings, we want more or we want less. Craving is the seed of suffering because it leads to clinging.

Clinging

Clinging or attachment to something is dependent upon our craving for it. With clinging firmly established, suffering is inevitable because all things are impermanent and unsatisfactory. Clinging leads to existence.

Existence

Existence—often referred to as "becoming"—is the arising into existence in one of the three realms of reality (Sensual Realm, Fine-material Realm, Formless Realm).

For beings who are blinded by ignorance, karma can be compared to a field, with consciousness as a seed and craving as moisture. With these conditions, consciousness becomes established in one of the three realms and leads to existence and rebirth.

Rebirth

Rebirth is dependent upon existence. It refers to the moment that consciousness is established in a womb, where the Five Aggregates and Six Senses manifest themselves.

Birth, or rebirth, inexorably leads to old age and death.

Old Age and Death

Death is dependent upon birth. Without birth there is no death.

The Buddha teaches that putting an end to ignorance thus prevents the making of karma (volitional actions). Without volition there can be no consciousness and, therefore, no mind, body, or six senses. Without senses there can be no contact. Without contact there are no feelings, no craving, no clinging or becoming. Without becoming there can be no birth and therefore no death. To put an end to ignorance, then, means to realize the true and lasting peace of the Deathless: Nirvana.

Right Intention
Page 42

Right Intention

Intention toward Renunciation

Craving is the source of suffering within ourselves and in the world. Craving is quelled, however, with the intention toward renunciation. Renunciation, which is the counterpart of attachment, applies to anything we may cling to, including not just material things, but relationships, sensual pleasures, opinions about the way things "should" be, and belief in a self that is everlasting and unchanging.

Renunciation does not mean living a life of absolute austerity, that is, giving up everything. The Buddha tried it and discovered that the approach does not work. Instead, the Buddha teaches to use only what is necessary and to do so without attachment.

Intention toward Good Will

Thoughts of anger and aversion, which can be about people, things, the weather, or anything at all, breed suffering. We can replace these harmful thoughts with those of good will—also called loving kindness—toward ourselves and others. We intend good will toward ourselves because, of course, we want to be happy. Furthermore, we understand that everyone wants to be happy.

With the intention toward good will, we guide the mind away from harmful thoughts and toward thoughts conducive to peace and calm, which come with the acceptance of the way things are.

Intention toward Harmlessness

Wishing for, or taking satisfaction in the suffering of others also leads to our suffering. Harmful thoughts—a view that someone should be punished, for example—go beyond anger because they become the basis of intention. When an intention is in place, action is likely to follow.

Our intention toward harmlessness proposes an atmosphere of safety for ourselves and others. It is the embodiment of compassion.

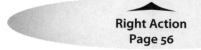

Right Action
Page 56

The Five Precepts

Abstaining from Killing

The precept against killing applies not just to the killing of human beings but to the killing of any being. We practice this precept with the intention that the people, animals, and all other living creatures that come into our lives be free from physical harm. On the subtlest of levels, where microbes are involved, for example, following this precept may be impossible. But what is important is the *intention* of offering safety to all beings everywhere and without discrimination.

Abstaining from Taking Things Not Given

This precept is more than just refraining from stealing. We understand that anything not given to us—implicitly or explicitly—belongs to someone else and, therefore, is to be left alone. We accept only what is given freely, without coercion or deceit, including intangible property as well, such as ideas.

Abstaining from Sexual Misconduct

The Buddha defined sexual misconduct as sexual abuse, extramarital affairs, and sexual relationships with underage people. Sexual misconduct has ill effects on ourselves and others. Sometimes they are immediate; sometimes they are unrealized for many years. When we undertake the precept to abstain from sexual misconduct, we make the intention to protect not only others but also ourselves from certain harm.

Abstaining from Lying

To practice Buddhism is to practice seeking the truth, that is, the true nature of reality. Any kind of lie, small or large, impedes our progress by bolstering delusion. A lie also places others at risk, at the very least by perpetuating delusion. But lies may also lead to physical and emotional harm to ourselves and others. To abstain from lying is to eliminate such potential dangers.

Abstaining from Intoxicants

Even in small amounts, using alcohol and recreational drugs may have a negative effect on our mindfulness and therefore our behavior. They may lead to the breaching of the other four precepts. To abstain from their use helps prevent mistakes that are potentially harmful to all beings, ourselves included.

Right Action
Page 57

The Ten Perfections

Generosity

With the practice of generosity we give to all beings without judgment or regard to worthiness. We give without expectation of anything in return. We give, not out a sense of plenty, but from what we have—even if all we have are best wishes. Although it is difficult to perfect, generosity is the easiest to start with because being generous is something we can do at any time. We can start with small offerings, gradually reinforcing the habit of giving until it becomes easier and easier. Generosity forms the foundation for the other perfections.

Virtue

With a virtuous life we offer safety to ourselves and to others. A virtuous person is nonthreatening in word and deed, speaks the truth and behaves in ways that are truly harmless. Treating others kindly is an act of generosity.

Renunciation

The idea that true happiness comes from letting go rather than from acquiring is at the heart of the Buddha's teachings. Renunciation sometimes refers to giving up things we are attached to and sometimes means just giving up the attachment while still retaining that thing in our lives.

Renunciation means not grasping after things and ideas, and being content with what we have. Renunciation does not mean giving up everything. It means giving up wanting things to be different. It means giving up all things that lead to suffering. Renunciation complements virtue and generosity.

Wisdom

With the perfection of wisdom, we can discern—that is, see and understand—what is just enough, what is virtuous, what is skillful. With wisdom we can understand what is harmful or beneficial to ourselves and others. We understand how greed, hatred, and delusion are the sources of suffering.

Energy

To make spiritual progress, especially with regard to the Ten Perfections, we need energy. With energy we can apply the persistent effort necessary to develop the qualities of a buddha. Spiritual practice is a full-time job, a way of life.   ➤

**Right Action
Continued**

The Ten Perfections

Patience

Patience implies tolerance and forbearance for the idiosyncrasies of others and the misfortunes of life. All things eventually change. Some things—situations, people, ourselves—change more slowly than others. Because of a deep understanding of the nature of reality, a buddha displays infinite patience with others.

Truthfulness

Truthfulness means being honest in our speech and in our thoughts. It means acting with integrity and without pretense. Truthfulness is a component of Right Speech and is one of the Five Precepts.

Resolution

With unshakable resolve we practice for the benefit of all beings. Resolution implies a constancy to our practice that is not affected by moods or events or the actions of others. Every day, moment to moment, we resolve to live by the Five Precepts and practice the Ten Perfections.

Loving Kindness

An awakened individual maintains a heart filled with loving kindness toward all beings, without regard to their disposition. With the perfection of kindness and good will, one has no enemies because one does not view anyone as "enemy." Rather, all beings are seen through eyes of compassion and, therefore, are treated with kindness.

Equanimity

Equanimity is the last perfection. After we develop the other nine, equanimity comes naturally. Equanimity is the quality of being perfectly balanced in all things. We are not blown about by the inevitable ups and downs of life but instead remain calm and thoughtful regardless of the situation.

We accept things as they are with an understanding that the past is unchangeable and the present is the workshop where future events can be influenced by our current actions.

Right Effort
Page 58

The Four Great Efforts

Effort to Avoid

With the Effort to Avoid, we guard against the arising of new unwholesome or negative thoughts. We are mindfully vigilant, always watching our thoughts as they present themselves, always on the lookout for thoughts that will carry us away from attention to the moment.

Effort to Overcome

If negative or unwholesome thoughts or afflictive emotions do arise, we strive to abandon them through the Effort to Overcome. From experience we know that these thoughts lead to suffering for ourselves and for those around us. We apply energy and effort to let them go and return to a state of equanimity.

Effort to Develop

With a mind free of negative thoughts, we can encourage the development of wholesome thoughts and emotions that have not yet arisen. Such development is accomplished through the application of loving kindness and compassion toward ourselves and others.

Effort to Maintain

After positive thoughts and emotions have arisen, we make an effort to maintain them. Maintenance is accomplished by sustaining a wholesome state of mind while guarding against the arising of negative thoughts and emotions.

Right Mindfulness
Page 59

The Four Foundations of Mindfulness

Mindfulness of the Body

The direct way to bring mindfulness to the body is to focus on the breath. We simply notice our breathing in and breathing out. We notice when the breath is long or short, deep or shallow. We are mindful that the breath arises and passes away—just as all conditioned phenomena do.

Mindfulness of the body can also focus on the four main postures: standing, walking, sitting, and lying down. In other words, we are mindful of all the positions and movements of the body during all activities.

The Buddha offers two more methods to bring mindfulness to the body. The first is to contemplate the unattractive aspects of the body and focus on its various constituents, including blood, hair, marrow, organs, sinews, pus, phlegm, and bile. The texts list 32 specific aspects in all. In earlier days, monks were encouraged to practice charnel meditation: They would visit a charnel ground, a place where bodies were disposed of. Here, they would contemplate bodies in various degrees of decomposition as a means of recognizing and accepting their own impermanence.

One also can be mindful of the body in reference to the Four Elements: earth, water, wind, and fire.

Mindfulness of Feelings

Feelings refer to pleasant, unpleasant, or neutral reactions to sense contact, as described in the Five Aggregates (p. 51). At any given moment, one of these feelings will arise and pass away to be replaced by another. With mindfulness we notice feelings as they arise and discern whether they are pleasant, unpleasant, or neutral. Then we can minimize their effects so we will not be carried away by them.

Mindfulness of the Mind

Mindfulness of the mind means being aware of the general condition of the mind itself as opposed to awareness of mental objects—thoughts, for example. The mind is the "watcher" of what's happening in both the inner and outer world. We understand a mind affected by greed, hatred, or delusion, or understand a mind *unaffected* by greed, hatred, or delusion. We understand a focussed, concentrated, and liberated mind, or a scattered, dull, or anxious mind. When any of these conditions arises, the mind recognizes it and doesn't get involved.   ➤

The Four Foundations of Mindfulness

Mindfulness of Mental Objects

A mental object is a thought or formation and is also one of the Five Aggregates (p. 51). Mindfulness of mental objects means to maintain bare awareness of the object. We note, for example, "This is a mind filled with anxiety" or "This is merely a thought." There is no judgment of right or wrong, no attempt to change things, no attachment such as "I am anxious." It is simply the observation of how these objects of mind arise and pass away. When we are mindful of mental objects we investigate those objects, taking them apart in order to see that they are impermanent, unsatisfactory, and of no substance.

A mental object—or mental quality—can be negative or positive, depending on our mood. In a sense, our moods give color to thoughts. Whereas mindfulness of the mind notes the color, mindfulness of mental objects notes the thought. Negative or unwholesome mental qualities are categorized as one of the Five Hindrances. Positive or wholesome mental qualities are categorized as one of the Seven Factors for Awakening.

Only one object can arise within the mind at any moment, although it often seems that many things are happening at once. During meditation we note with bare attention the state of mind as it arises. Then we bring that quality into full awareness as the object of meditation.

For example, when the breath is the object of meditation, we notice how it rises, pauses for a while, then passes away. Then we notice its quality, its texture, and whether it's long or short or deep or shallow. The same examination can take place with mental objects. If the mind is filled with doubt, we peel away the layers as we discern just what the nature of doubt really is. We don't let the mind wander to what it is we are doubtful about, which is equivalent to letting the mind wander away from the breath. Rather, we stay with the quality itself. What is doubt? What causes it? What can it do? Why is it called a hindrance? What can be done to counter it (rather than pretend it isn't there)?

The Four Elements

Page 88
Four Elements

Right Mindfulness
Page 87

The Four Elements

All physical forms can be examined in terms of the elements—or properties—of earth, water, wind, and fire. To the human body we can add the additional properties of space and consciousness.

Viewing matter in these terms predates Buddhism, and the elements have meaning beyond their literal translations. In ancient times it was how people explained physical phenomena.

It is said that the Buddha and other *arahants* (holy ones) who were able to perform certain feats such as levitation and moving through solid objects did so by mentally manipulating the elements.

In meditation we can explore how the elements interact with one another.

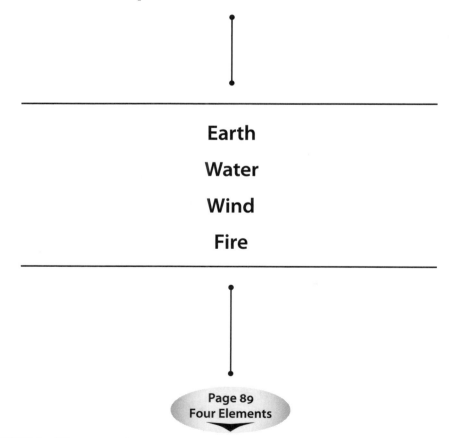

Earth

Water

Wind

Fire

Page 89
Four Elements

Right Mindfulness
Page 88

The Four Elements

Earth

The earth element is that of solidity, hardness, and weight. The body is composed of solid particles held together by the water element; supported, strengthened, and moved by the wind element; and preserved and sustained by the fire element.

Water

Coolness, cohesion, and fluidity are characteristics of the water element. This element binds the earth element, which, in turn, keeps the water element in place. Water also is supported by the wind element and sustained by the fire element.

Wind

Wind is the motion element and is characterized by movement, strengthening, and supporting. Wind supports the body, giving it strength and the ability to move. It rests in the earth element, is held in place by the water element, and is nourished by the fire element.

Fire

Heat is the characteristic of the fire element. This element digests food, produces energy, and preserves and sustains the other elements. It rests in the earth element, is held in place by the water element, and is supported by the wind element.

Right Mindfulness
Page 61

The Seven Factors for Awakening

Mindfulness

Mindfulness is the primary factor for awakening. All the other factors are based on mindfulness; it is the necessary ingredient for practice, both in formal meditation and in day-to-day activities. Mindfulness brings us into the present. When we are mindful, we know what we are doing (including thinking and speaking) *as* we are doing it.

Mindfulness means remembering to bring attention to the breath or other object of meditation. The practice of mindfulness is to remember the instructions over and over throughout the day.

Investigation of the Dharma

What leads to suffering? What leads to happiness? What is skillful? What is unskillful? Wise reflection on questions such as these—with the intention of investigating the true nature of things—is the core of this factor for awakening.

To investigate the Dharma is to use discernment as a means to see clearly the way things are and not be misled by delusion. Investigation through the faculty of discernment is an important complement to mindfulness.

Energy

Maintaining a state of mindfulness and ongoing discernment calls for effort. Making the effort to initiate and sustain these wholesome mental states requires energy. Energy for our bodies comes from the food we eat. Energy for our minds comes from a deep resolve to end our suffering and the conviction that we are on the right path.

Rapture

Rapture is state of enthusiasm and joy that is not dependent upon external things or events. It arises in the absence of the Five Hindrances—desire, ill will, sloth and torpor, restlessness and remorse, and doubt—and is subtle and not easily recognized if the mind is distracted. Discerning rapture requires a mind that is tranquil, calm, and focused on the present moment. ➤

The Seven Factors for Awakening

Tranquility

Tranquility, or serenity, is a state of calm in which peacefulness and ease predominate. Agitation, restlessness, and worry slip away.

A tranquil mind is a spacious mind, uncluttered by useless or distracting thoughts and emotions. Within this spaciousness, the other factors for awakening can develop unimpeded.

Concentration

Concentration is also referred to as one-pointedness of mind. It is the ability to remain focused on the breath or other object of meditation. Mindfulness brings the mind to the present moment. Concentration keeps it there.

Insight into the true nature of things—that all conditioned things are impermanent, unsatisfactory, and impersonal—arises within the concentrated mind.

Equanimity

Equanimity is evenness of temperament, the quality of being unmoved in the midst of the vicissitudes of life. It is the quelling of the passions, both positive and negative. Equanimity is the complete acceptance of the way things are, without judgment or afflictive emotions.

A mind filled with equanimity is one that neither dwells on the past nor becomes anxious with the future. Equanimity should not be confused with being apathetic or uncaring, however. Negative mental formations have no place to grow in a mind composed of equanimity.

The mind filled with equanimity remains in the present, where—with the aid of concentration and wisdom—it experiences liberation from all conditioned phenomena.

Right Concentration
Page 64

The Five Hindrances

Sensual Desire

When the mind is filled with sensual desire—for pleasant sights, sounds, smells, tastes, things to touch, and things to think about—it grasps at what is desired and is mesmerized by it. Imagine a bowl of water swirling with iridescent paints. As beautiful as it is to look at, clarity is obscured. The antidote to desire is to contemplate the repulsive and repugnant (impermanent and ultimately unsatisfactory) nature of things.

Ill Will

Ill will results from anger and aversion. Water churning on the fires of hatred and anger reflects no image. The antidote to ill will is to offer loving kindness and compassion to oneself and all beings.

Sloth and Torpor

Sloth and torpor are mental dullness and drowsiness. Water choked with weeds evokes the idea of sloth and torpor. The antidote to these hindrances is effort and exertion.

Restlessness and Remorse

Restlessness is a form of excitement and agitation, an impatience with how things are. Remorse is worry and guilt, usually as a result of moral transgressions. Water whipped by a strong wind represents this compound hindrance. Contemplating tranquility and equanimity counteracts restlessness and worry.

Doubt

Doubt is an expression of uncertainty regarding the teachings and the practice of the Dharma. An unsettled mind obscured by doubt offers no more clarity of vision than water viewed in darkness. Striving to see things how they really are, having faith in the teachings of the Buddha, and thinking about the benefits of practice illuminate the darkness and are the antidotes to doubt.

Right Concentration
Page 65

The Four Sublime Abidings

Loving Kindness

Abiding within a mind filled with loving kindness, we spread thoughts of good will in all directions with the intention that all beings be happy, peaceful, and content. We include ourselves and those we may view as enemies or as otherwise undeserving. Loving kindness counters feelings of ill will and hatred.

Compassion

When we dwell within a mind filled with compassion, we empathize with the pain and suffering of all sentient beings (including ourselves). Our wish for all beings is that they be free from all forms of suffering and harm. Compassion counters the afflictive thoughts of hostility and harm.

Appreciation

To dwell with appreciation means to take delight in the achievements, health, and good fortune of all others. When we abide within a mind filled with appreciation, we counter feelings of envy and jealousy. Appreciation is sometimes referred to as sympathetic joy.

Equanimity

Equanimity reaches deep into the nature of karma. With equanimity comes the understanding that we are unequivocally responsible for our actions, past, present, and future.

Further, we maintain the calm acceptance of the results of our past actions coupled with the understanding that the only actions that matter are those that occur in the present.

When we cultivate and remain in a mind filled with equanimity we see that all beings are no different from ourselves both in their faults and in their desire for happiness. Then we can radiate equanimity in all directions to all beings so they, too, may be calm and accepting.

Equanimity counters anxiety and restlessness.

**Right Concentration
Page 66**

Tranquility and the Jhanas

The Four Jhanas

In the first jhana, or meditative absorption, the Five Hindrances are completely abandoned. We are free—temporarily at least—from desire, aversion, restlessness and remorse, sloth and torpor, and doubt. We are mentally alert and physically energized.

Five mental qualities remain, however: the placing of attention on a meditation object, the sustaining of attention on the object, rapture, happiness, and one-pointedness. To place attention on an object is to initially grab hold of it. Then we maintain attention on the object. These are considered two distinct qualities. A mind that is one-pointed is stable and still, not moving from place to place.

In the second jhana, the placing and holding of attention fall away. Rapture, happiness, and one-pointedness remain.

When rapture falls away, one enters the third jhana. Happiness and one-pointedness remain.

In the fourth jhana, even happiness disappears. What remains is a completely purified form of concentration and equanimity.

The four jhanas are associated with the Fine-material, or Form, Realm (see Rebirth and the Planes of Existence, p. 52.)

The Immaterial Attainments

Four levels of successively refined states are attainable beyond the first four jhanas. They are the Immaterial, or Formless, attainments. They are not numbered as such but are named for their objects of meditation. Unlike the jhanas, in which the meditator places attention on a specific tangible object such as the breath, a symbol, or a bodily sensation, in these refined states the objects of meditation have no form at all. They are infinite space, infinite consciousness, nothingness, and neither perception nor non-perception. These attainments correspond to the Immaterial Realm, in which matter has become nonexistent and only mental processes remain.

Beyond these attainments another extremely subtle and profound state of meditation is possible: the cessation of feeling and perception. These attainments are not the same as Nirvana, the liberation from endless rounds of suffering, but they are part of the step-by-step process to liberation. At least some experience with the first four jhanas is necessary to obtain the clarity, energy, and radically different perspective necessary to let go of worldly concerns.

Appendices

Appendix A: The Maps at a Glance

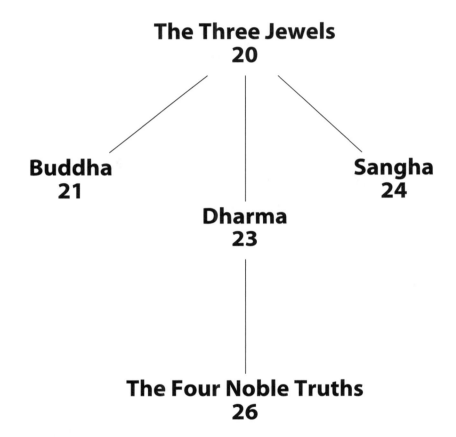

The Three Jewels
20

Buddha
21

Sangha
24

Dharma
23

The Four Noble Truths
26

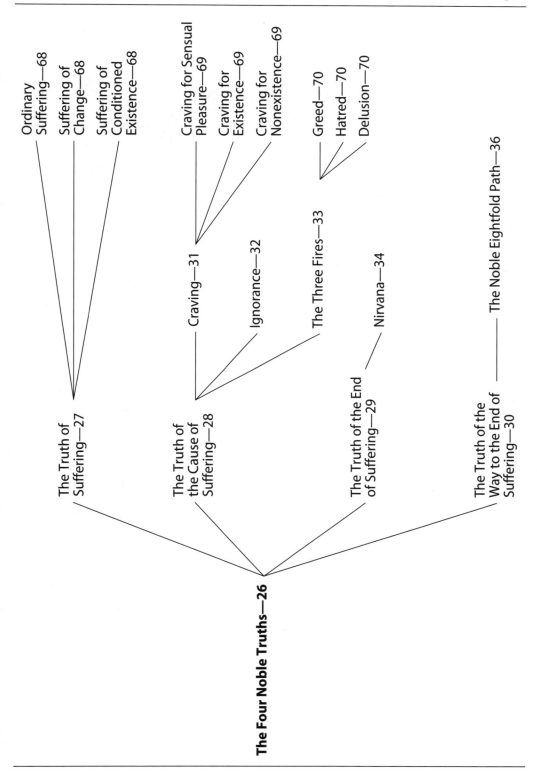

The Four Noble Truths—26

The Truth of Suffering—27
- Ordinary Suffering—68
- Suffering of Change—68
- Suffering of Conditioned Existence—68

The Truth of the Cause of Suffering—28
- Craving—31
  - Craving for Sensual Pleasure—69
  - Craving for Existence—69
  - Craving for Nonexistence—69
- Ignorance—32
- The Three Fires—33
  - Greed—70
  - Hatred—70
  - Delusion—70

The Truth of the End of Suffering—29
- Nirvana—34

The Truth of the Way to the End of Suffering—30
- The Noble Eightfold Path—36

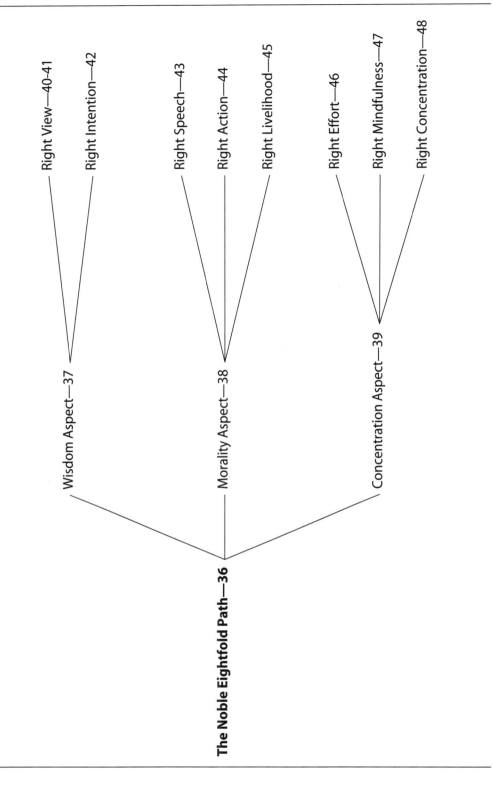

The Noble Eightfold Path—36

Wisdom Aspect—37
- Right View—40-41
- Right Intention—42

Morality Aspect—38
- Right Speech—43
- Right Action—44
- Right Livelihood—45

Concentration Aspect—39
- Right Effort—46
- Right Mindfulness—47
- Right Concentration—48

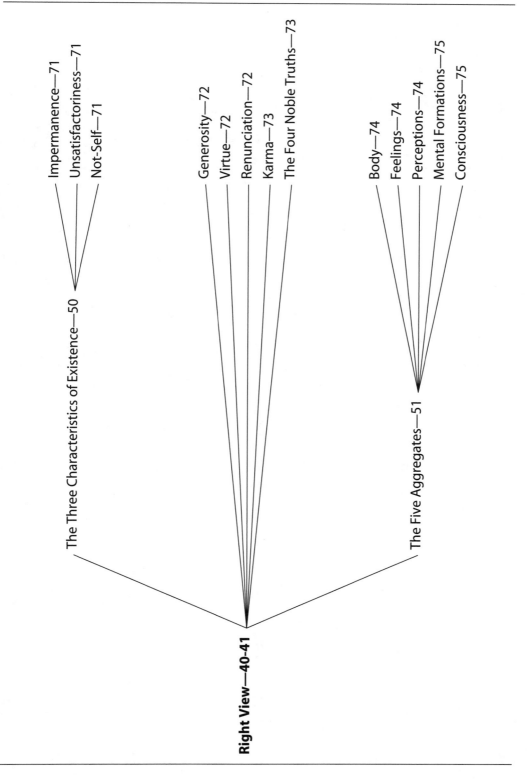

The Three Characteristics of Existence—50

- Impermanence—71
- Unsatisfactoriness—71
- Not-Self—71

Right View—**40-41**

- Generosity—72
- Virtue—72
- Renunciation—72
- Karma—73
- The Four Noble Truths—73

The Five Aggregates—51

- Body—74
- Feelings—74
- Perceptions—74
- Mental Formations—75
- Consciousness—75

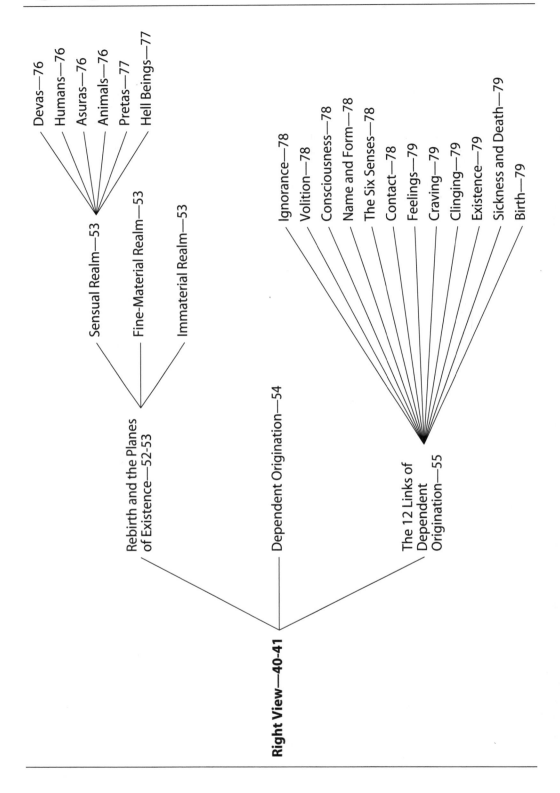

Right View—40-41

Rebirth and the Planes of Existence—52-53

Sensual Realm—53
- Devas—76
- Humans—76
- Asuras—76
- Animals—76
- Pretas—77
- Hell Beings—77

Fine-Material Realm—53

Immaterial Realm—53

Dependent Origination—54

The 12 Links of Dependent Origination—55
- Ignorance—78
- Volition—78
- Consciousness—78
- Name and Form—78
- The Six Senses—78
- Contact—78
- Feelings—79
- Craving—79
- Clinging—79
- Existence—79
- Sickness and Death—79
- Birth—79

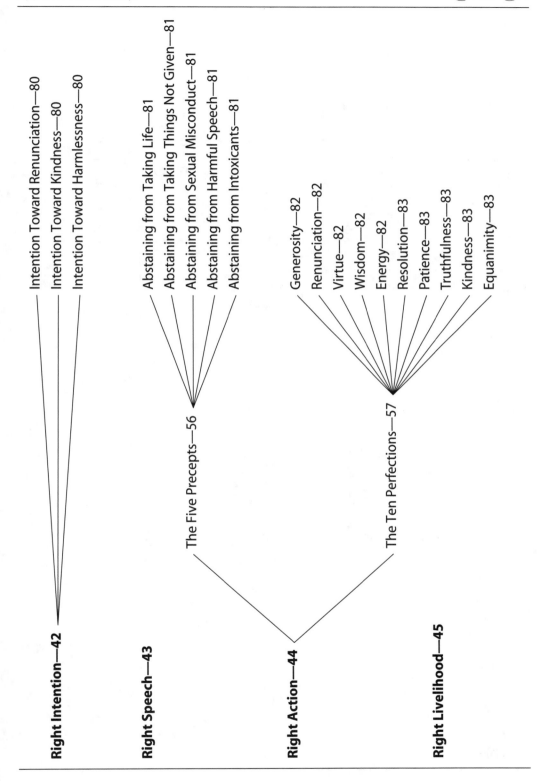

Right Intention—42
- Intention Toward Renunciation—80
- Intention Toward Kindness—80
- Intention Toward Harmlessness—80

Right Speech—43

The Five Precepts—56
- Abstaining from Taking Life—81
- Abstaining from Taking Things Not Given—81
- Abstaining from Sexual Misconduct—81
- Abstaining from Harmful Speech—81
- Abstaining from Intoxicants—81

Right Action—44

The Ten Perfections—57
- Generosity—82
- Renunciation—82
- Virtue—82
- Wisdom—82
- Energy—82
- Resolution—83
- Patience—83
- Truthfulness—83
- Kindness—83
- Equanimity—83

Right Livelihood—45

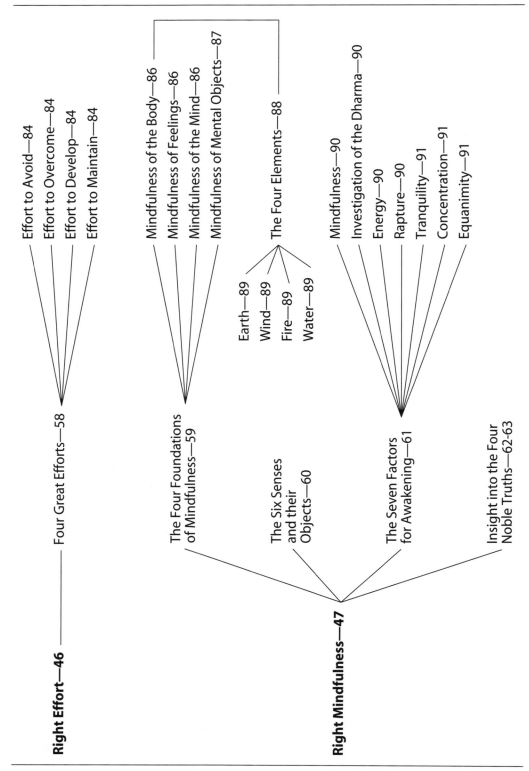

Right Effort—46 ———————— Four Great Efforts—58

Effort to Avoid—84
Effort to Overcome—84
Effort to Develop—84
Effort to Maintain—84

The Four Foundations of Mindfulness—59

Mindfulness of the Body—86
Mindfulness of Feelings—86
Mindfulness of the Mind—86
Mindfulness of Mental Objects—87

The Four Elements—88

Earth—89
Wind—89
Fire—89
Water—89

The Six Senses and their Objects—60

Right Mindfulness—47

The Seven Factors for Awakening—61

Mindfulness—90
Investigation of the Dharma—90
Energy—90
Rapture—90
Tranquility—91
Concentration—91
Equanimity—91

Insight into the Four Noble Truths—62-63

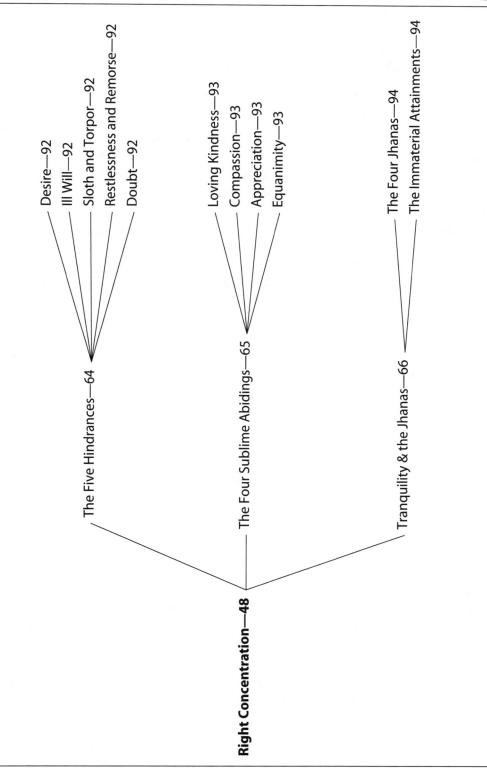

The Five Hindrances—64
- Desire—92
- Ill Will—92
- Sloth and Torpor—92
- Restlessness and Remorse—92
- Doubt—92

The Four Sublime Abidings—65
- Loving Kindness—93
- Compassion—93
- Appreciation—93
- Equanimity—93

Tranquility & the Jhanas—66
- The Four Jhanas—94
- The Immaterial Attainments—94

Right Concentration—48

Appendix B: Meditation and its Importance in Daily Life

Meditation has gained popularity as way to relieve stress and even control a degree of physical and emotional pain. In a Buddhist context, however, there is more to meditation than just sitting quietly with the eyes closed and more reasons to meditate than simple stress relief. The purpose of Buddhist meditation is to gain insight into ourselves and the world.

Insight is not unusual. At any moment we can gain understanding about a particular situation or realize a solution to a nagging problem. For a Buddhist, however, insight refers to gaining a deep understanding of the true nature of reality. Such understanding is the real and palpable knowledge that all conditioned things are impermanent, unsatisfactory, and without an enduring, changeless substance. Anything that comes into existence—be it a country or continent, planet or solar system, pain or pleasure, individual or relationship, idea or emotional state—will go out of existence. Anything that can go out of existence cannot bring true and lasting happiness. To believe otherwise is delusion. Delusion, along with grasping and aversion, is one of the Three Fires. These fires are the causes of all suffering in the world.

This is the reality discovered by the Buddha. In meditation we can discover this reality for ourselves.

The process of meditation begins with Right Effort. The traditional posture for meditation is cross-legged, although not necessarily full or half-lotus. Sitting in a straight-back chair or kneeling while propped on a short bench are also good postures if sitting cross-legged is not possible. The idea is to fix yourself in an upright position and stay there. Beginners can start with 10- or 15-minute sessions. With daily practice it's eventually possible to sit for an hour or more with little or no discomfort—or, if there is discomfort, it becomes less and less prominent in the mind. Consistency is important. The body and the the mind must get used to the idea of frequent and prolonged meditation.

After you are seated, take note of your breath as it goes in and out without trying to control it. You can focus your attention at the tip of your nose, feeling the sensations as the breath passes in and out. Or, you can focus on the rise and fall of your abdomen. You will find that your mind wanders. Just return to the breath.

Initially, you will notice that the mind cannot, will not, be empty. At first you may see chaos. Maybe you will try to run from it. Stick with it anyway. You will soon recognize it for what it is: your normal state of affairs. It's what's going on whether or not you are paying attention, just as breathing goes on whether or not you are paying attention. Just stay with the breath.

Patience is one of the Ten Perfections. Over a short time you likely will notice small differences in your outlook, but real progress happens with sustained practice. Patiently return to your meditation area each day, and patiently return again and again to the breath.

During meditation, Right Mindfulness is what keeps you anchored to your breath, what keeps you from straying, what keeps you from getting involved in what's "outside." Imagine you are in a fenced area with a child playing nearby. Outside the fence are any number of distractions and dangers. You, as the parent, are intent on the child. You know the distractions are there, but the child is safe because of the fence. The child is the breath. The fence is mindfulness. And you are simply the well-trained watcher, without opinion, without concern, and without grasping at the distractions.

Thoughts arise and pass away only to be replaced by other thoughts. As they arise, take note of them and let them go. Resist the temptation to become involved and carried away. A deep-space telescope "sees" what it's pointed at, but in no way does it get involved. Such is the well-trained mind.

Tranquility and Insight, also referred to as *Samatha* and *Vipassana* (*Shamatha* and *Vipashyana* in Sanskrit) are the results of applying Right Effort and Right Mindfulness. Yet, meditation presents us with a baffling challenge. If the idea is to focus on the breath, how do all these other wonderful things happen?. Where do all the understanding and insight come from?

With sustained concentration tranquility arises. A tranquil mind is the laboratory in which we can discover and touch the Four Noble Truths and the lessons they contain. Imagine taking a look at a thought or emotional state and examining it much as a chemist would examine a meal to determine the number of calories and nutritional value of each of its elements. If losing weight is your goal, then you will be very particular about the quality and quantity of the food you ingest. A well-balanced diet is conducive to good health. The same is true for thoughts. With practice you can train the mind to control the content and quality of your thoughts. Some tools you can use for training the mind are the Four Great Efforts. Others are offering Loving Kindness and Compassion— offered not just to others, but to yourself as well, especially yourself.

With careful examination of the breath we can see how it arises and passes away, arises and passes away. We can see how the breath is a microcosm of the body itself. And we can see then how the breath can be a microcosm of everything within the universe. These understandings comprise insight.

Insight contains its own kind of paradox. When it arises in the mind and you are alert to it, you will see it. For a moment there is a flurry of excitement. But any insight that arises is a conditioned phenomenon. As such, it will pass. Its importance and brilliance will grow dim. But in its place will be a subtle change to your understanding of how things are.

It is through this careful, patient, and sustained examination of the breath that a well-trained mind is developed. Insights arise in a still, observant, well-trained mind. You then can take these insights into your daily life, where they can make a real difference.

Appendix C: Theravada, Mahayana, and Vajrayana Buddhism

Before he became the Buddha, the Perfectly Enlightened One, Siddhartha Gautama sought only this: the cause of suffering and the end of suffering. He sought the way out of the cycle of *samsara*, the endless cycle of birth, death, pain, lamentation, grief, and despair to which all human beings were—and continue to be—subject.

On the night of his awakening his objective sparkled as clearly in his mind as the stars above him. His innumerable realizations of his own past and future lives, as well as the far-reaching effects of karma, took form as the constellation he called the Four Noble Truths.

Soon, the Buddha set out to teach others how they, too, could realize full awakening. Many hundreds of thousands who followed him did so and became *arahants* (holy ones, fully awakened but not buddhas), some immediately upon hearing the words of the Buddha.

During 45 years of teaching, the Buddha's discourses were mainly concerned with the truth of suffering and the path of practice leading to the end of suffering. Were someone to put a question to him regarding philosophical matters irrelevant to the practice, he would explain that such knowledge was of little value compared to the knowledge of what was skillful in bringing one's own suffering to an end in this lifetime.

Before he died, the Buddha did not appoint a successor. Rather, he declared that the Dharma, together with the Vinaya, the monastic code of discipline, would be the teacher after his passing.

Soon after his death in 483 BCE, many hundreds of arahants within the Sangha gathered to recite the teachings and reach a consensus on what were in fact the words of the Buddha himself. Memorized and codified, the teachings were systematically transmitted orally until they were finally written down in on palm leaves in Sri Lanka in the early part of the first century BCE.

Theravada and the Pali Canon

The teachings were first written in the language of Pali, the language of the common people of that era, so they are known as the Pali Canon. The Pali Canon has three parts, collectively referred to as the *Tripitaka* (three baskets). First is the *Vinaya Pitaka*, the monastic code as taught by the Buddha. The second, the *Sutta Pitaka,* contains the Dharma discourses of the Buddha. Third is the *Abhidhamma Pitaka,* a collection of commentaries and other scholarly works.

As Buddhism spread throughout India and outward (migrations known as the Northern and Southern Transmissions), disagreements arose within diverse sanghas regarding the interpretations of some of the teachings and monastic rules. These disagreements resulted in several schisms. During the early growth of Buddhism some 18 schools began. Of those, only one, the Theravada (Doctrine of the Elders) School, remains. It relies solely on the Pali Canon as its reference. Later accretions are generally not included. Theravada is associated with the Southern Transmission, which reached Thailand, Myanmar, and Sri Lanka.

Mahayana

The Buddha taught others the way to freedom from suffering. The path to awakening was considered a personal journey. Becoming an arahant—not a buddha—was the ideal. Although some people might have taken a vow to become a buddha, buddhahood in and of itself was not the goal.

Around the beginning of the Common Era there arose a new ideal, that of the *bodhisattva,* a buddha-to-be. The *ideal* bodhisattva is one who, out of limitless compassion, puts off realization of Nirvana until *all beings* are freed from the wheel of suffering. The goal is buddhahood, attained through moral development and selfless work on behalf of all beings. The bodhisattva *chooses* to remain in samsara, being reborn again and again until the work is done.

With the development of the bodhisattva ideal came the second major Buddhist school: the Mahayana, the Greater Vehicle.

To further distinguish themselves from the many other schools, the Mahayanists referred to other lineages as Hinayana, the Lesser, Low, or Common Vehicle. Mahayana is associated with the Northern Transmission, which includes Nepal, Bhutan, Russia, Tibet, Mongolia, China, Japan (Zen), Vietnam, and Korea.

When Buddhism entered China, the Pali Canon was translated into ancient Chinese. But it has since been superseded by texts introduced by many of the great sages who influenced Buddhist thinking over the millennia.

Vajrayana

A still later development within the Mahayana was the *Vajrayana,* the Diamond Vehicle. Whereas Theravada and Mahayana teachings are readily available to anyone who chooses to hear them, Vajrayana teachings are set apart by two important factors: *esoteric* and *tantric.* Vajrayana is considered a rapid path to full awakening and therefore dangerous to one not fully mature and completely prepared for it. The teachings are esoteric because they are closely guarded and transmitted through a strict and profound guru–student relationship. Only in that way can they be effective.

Tantra involves a variety of techniques that expedite the practitioner's journey. Among these techniques are the use of *mantras* (sacred phrases), *mudras* (hand positions), *mandalas* (geometric images), rituals and ritualistic objects, and *yoga* (of which there are many kinds beyond the popular exercise technique). Also within tantra is a vast cosmology and the recognition of a panoply of deities. Of the thousands of *suttas* (discourses) in the Pali Canon, only a handful still remain in the Vajrayana teachings.

Many schools are within the Vajrayana tradition, and although not specific to Tibet, it is most associated with Tibetan Buddhism.

Glossary

Aggregate A collection of things or components. Buddhist doctrine states that a person is composed of five aggregates, i.e., five collections of things that are at the same time distinct and interdependent.

Anatta *See* Not-self

Anicca *See* Impermanence

Arahant A fully awakened being, free of the Ten Fetters that bind one to the world and whose realization of Nirvana is complete.

Asura A powerful and ill-tempered inhabitant of the Asura Realm and sometimes referred to as titans or jealous gods.

Birth *See* Rebirth

Bodhisattva A buddha-to-be. A person destined for awakening for the sake of all beings.

Body The material or form aspect of name-and-form, i.e., mind and body. One of the Five Aggregates

Buddha (the) The Awakened One, the Knower of the Worlds. The Buddha discovered the Four Noble Truths and taught about the causes of suffering in the world and how to bring that suffering to an end. *See also* Tathagata.

Compassion Empathy with the pain and suffering of all beings.

Concentration One-pointedness of mind. The ability to bring the mind into sharp focus on an object of meditation.

Consciousness The awareness that arises at one of the six sense doors, i.e., eye consciousness, ear consciousness, nose consciousness, tongue consciousness, body or touch consciousness, and mind consciousness.

Contact The point at which consciousness arises between, for example, the eye and an object of sight.

Craving *(tanha)* One of the primary causes, along with ignorance, of all suffering in the world. Craving is a thirst for things to be different from what they are.

Delusion The inability to see things as they truly are, i.e., that all things are impermanent, unsatisfactory, and not-self. See also Ignorance.

Dependent origination The doctrine that all things come into existence as a result of an infinitely regressive chain of causes and conditions.

Desire A leaning toward any form of sensual pleasure, desire is considered a hindrance to meditation and spiritual growth. The one desire considered worthy by the Buddha is the desire for awakening and the end of suffering. *See also* Craving

Deva An inhabitant one of the six planes of the Heaven Realm and of the Fine-material and Immaterial Realms, a radiant being.

Dharma Capitalized, the collective teachings of the Buddha. Dharma can also mean "truth," "things," "phenomena," or "the way things are."

Dukkha Any form of dissatisfaction, including birth, death, sickness, despair, dissatisfaction, irritation, lack, unpleasant situation or association, etc., so long as there is the least desire for things to be otherwise.

Eightfold Path *See* Noble Eightfold Path

Equanimity The state of being calm and detached regardless of the situation. With equanimity comes the understanding that there are certain consequences of one's past actions (karma) that can't be denied or avoided and therefore should be accepted responsibly. Equanimity also implies equal treatment of others regardless of one's feelings toward them.

Feeling One of the Five Aggregates. A feeling is either pleasant, unpleasant, or neutral.

Four Noble Truths Discovered, fully comprehended, realized, and developed by the Buddha upon his awakening: suf-fering, the cause of suffering, the possible end of suffering, and the means to the end of suffering.

Ignorance *(avijja)* The root cause of all suffering in the world. Because of ignorance of the Four Noble Truths, greed, hatred, and delusion take hold. *See also* Delusion.

Impermanence *(anicca)* The doctrine that all conditioned things are impermanent and therefore lead to suffering.

Insight *(vipassana)* The penetrating knowledge of the true nature of things, i.e., that all conditioned things are impermanent, unsatisfactory, and not-self. Also an experiential understanding of the Four Noble Truths.

Jhana Meditative absorption. When plural, progressively deeper stages of absorption brought about by one-pointed and unwavering concentration on an object of meditation.

Karma *(kamma)* Volitional action. Any action done with intention, regardless of how slight the action or that the intention was unrecognized.

Law of Conditionality The doctrine that states the relationship between a thing or event and its causes and conditions. Without causes and conditions, nothing can exist. Stated as: When this is, that is; from the arising of this comes the arising of that; when this isn't, that isn't; from the stopping of this comes the stopping of that.

Mahayana The Greater Vehicle, one of the three major branches of Buddhism and part of the Northern Transmission, which includes Nepal, Bhutan, Russia, Tibet, Mongolia, China, Japan, Vietnam, and Korea. Zen is part of the Mahayana tradition. *Compare with* Theravada and Vajrayana.

Mental formation Will directed toward a perception. Anger, joy, sorrow, and happiness are mental formations. A thought. *See also* Will and Volition.

Mental object Anything that is held within or is part of the mind, including feelings, perceptions, mental formations, and consciousness.

Mind The mental or name aspect of name-and-form. Includes feelings, perceptions, mental formations, and consciousness.

Mindfulness The quality of awareness and the ability to bring bare attention to an object.

Nama-rupa *See* Name-and-form.

Name-and-form The mental and material parts of a being. Also Nama-rupa, mind and body.

Noble Eightfold Path The forth of the Four Noble Truths, the means to the end of suffering: Right View, Right Intention, Right Speech, Right Action, Right Livelihood, Right Effort, Right Mindfulness, Right Concentration

Not-self *(anatta)* The doctrine that nothing has a discrete, unchanging , and everlasting essence. Because they are always changing, the Five Aggregates that comprise a person—together or separately—cannot be construed as one's essential "self."

Pali Canon The discourses, commentaries, and monastic code of the Buddha and the scriptural basis of Theravada Buddhism. Also called the *Tripitaka* (three baskets), or simply the Pali, it was first written in the Pali language in Sri Lanka about 500 years after the Buddha's death.

Pali Scriptural and liturgical language of Theravada Buddhism.

Perception The recognition and labeling of objects as they arise into consciousness.

Precept A rule or guideline intended to regulate behavior.

Preta An inhabitant of the Preta Realm, an insatiable being, also called a hungry ghost.

Rapture A state of enthusiasm and joy not dependent on an external stimulus but brought about as a result of the absence the Five Hindrances.

Rebirth The moment consciousness is established in a womb. Rebirth inevitably leads to death, which, as a result of one's karma, leads once again to rebirth.

Samadhi *See* Concentration

Samatha *See* Tranquility

Samsara The endless cycle of suffering through innumerable rebirths.

Sangha Community of monks and nuns, past and present, who have or are following the way of the Buddha. Sometimes used as a casual reference to any Buddhist community, including laity.

Sanskrit Classical language of ancient India, and the scriptural and liturgical language of Mahayana Buddhism.

Sila *See* Virtue

Tathagata (the) The one who is "thus gone" or "thus come." The Buddha's reference to himself.

Theravada The Doctrine or Way of the Elders. The branch of Buddhism known as the Southern Transmission, which includes Thailand, Myanmar, and Sri Lanka. *Compare with* Mahayana and Vajrayana.

Tranquility A state of mind where peace and calm predominate.

Triple Gem The Buddha, the Dharma, and the Sangha. Also called the Three Jewels.

Unsatisfactoriness *(dukkha)* One of three inherent conditions of all things. The doctrine that all conditioned things, because they are impermanent and not-

self, are inevitably unsatisfactory.

Vajrayana The Diamond Vehicle, branch of Mahayana Buddhism most often associated with Tibet. *Compare with* Mahayana and Theravada.

Vipassana *See* Insight

Virtue Upright and moral behavior. Along with generosity, the foundation of Buddhist ethics.

Volition The use of one's will to direct the mind toward what is good, bad, or neutral.

Will The mental faculty by which one forms an intention.

Index

If you would like to order copies of this
book, please visit

www.paramipress.com

Or write to

Parami Press
13023 NE Hwy. 99, Suite 7, #193
Vancouver, WA 98686

Five percent of the net proceeds of the first print-
ing of this book will go to Vimutti Monastery

If you would like to make a donation to Vimutti
Monastery Please visit
www.vimutti.org.nz